'Arielle's groundbreaking book Practical Miracles: Choices that Heal and Build Resilience *brings together her incredible knowledge and expertise in NLP amassed from years of client work and practitioner courses, the latest scientific research into the mind-body connection, and her own unique insights into the causation of stress, anxiety, and ultimately disease. Arielle has distilled this information into an easy-to-understand and practical solution-focused book that is a must for anyone wanting to attract more peace, health, and the occasional miracle into their lives.'*
Karl Dawson, Hay House author and creator of *Matrix Reimprinting*

'Arielle has an elegant way of enabling you to understand her thinking clearly and simply, creating a space and a place where you will choose to 'do' the techniques offered. Once the shifts have been experienced you will choose to do more. All of the data offered is supported by an evidence-based structure, giving it great credibility. All you have to do is read it and do it... Become Me-sponsible.'
**Kevin Laye, author, international trainer and speaker,
Harley Street therapist, and director of Dolby Sound**

'While making The Living Matrix *documentary, I met Arielle to film her incredibly powerful story about healing her own brain tumor. Practical Miracles gives you the full story of how she did that. It's a must-read for anyone serious about mind-body healing.'*
**Harry Massey, founder of Nutri-energetics Systems,
The Living Matrix movie and the Choice Point Movement**

'Practical Miracles is a book that places, in a manner accessible to everyone, some of the most groundbreaking thinking in the world of health and physiology. A hundred years from now, when Arielle's ideas have at last become mainstream, the world will look back at the medicine of 2012 with the same horror as we do that of the Dark Ages.'
Alexander Asseily, founder and chairman of Jawbone; founder of State

'Arielle funnels an extensive understanding of current research into useful applications for everyday life. This book builds a bridge between theoretical insights and practical ways to help ourselves NOW.'
Michael Grinder, pioneer developer of NLP and non-verbal communication

'As I work mainly with PhD-educated scientists, conveying ideas to people in a logical and intellectual way is important. I really appreciate how the concepts and exercises in this book are communicated as a metaphorical, flowing story. The 'play on words' and the different dimensions of language add a poetic element to this educative and thought-provoking read.'

Suzanne Lovell, biotechnology operations and HR for organizations including The Institute of Cancer Research, ArQule (UK) Ltd and Inpharmatica, and consultant to a range of biotechnology companies

'This inspiring book will bring you blessings as it deepens your understanding, renews your spirit, and strengthens your belief and trust in yourself. It provides a very sensitive and practical explanation of how the mind works, and how every thought you have affects the healing process. Take time to reflect on each point and rediscover your known and unknown strengths.'

Simon Xavier Guerrand-Hermès, chairman,
Guerrand-Hermès Foundation for Peace

'Practical Miracles presents a broad spectrum of approaches that can be used to improve your life, health, and happiness. Arielle's unique concept of thought clouds helps in healing stressful emotions and increasing mindfulness. As they say in AA: "it works if you work it."'

Brian Van der Horst, former director, NLP Institute for Advanced Studies, San Francisco and Paris; columnist for *New Realities, Practical Psychology, Playboy, The Village Voice*. Now Paris bureau chief, *Integral Leadership Review*

'There are few people who wouldn't benefit from reading this helpful, informative, and insightful book. Just reading it will inspire you to a new level of consciousness about mind, body, and spirit. Practising this approach will not only assist healing, but act as preventive medicine.'

Dr Satish Chadha MS, FRCS, MRCO, DRCO, INLPTA Certified Trainer in NLP, and American Board of Hypnotherapy Certified Trainer in Hypnosis

Practical Miracles

Practical Miracles

CHOICES THAT HEAL AND BUILD RESILIENCE

ARIELLE ESSEX

HAY HOUSE

Australia • Canada • Hong Kong • India
South Africa • United Kingdom • United States

First published and distributed in the United Kingdom by:
Hay House UK Ltd, 292B Kensal Rd, London W10 5BE. Tel.: (44) 20 8962 1230;
Fax: (44) 20 8962 1239. www.hayhouse.co.uk

Published and distributed in the United States of America by:
Hay House, Inc., PO Box 5100, Carlsbad, CA 92018-5100. Tel.: (1) 760 431 7695 or
(800) 654 5126; Fax: (1) 760 431 6948 or (800) 650 5115.
www.hayhouse.com

Published and distributed in Australia by:
Hay House Australia Ltd, 18/36 Ralph St, Alexandria NSW 2015. Tel.: (61) 2 9669
4299; Fax: (61) 2 9669 4144. www.hayhouse.com.au

Published and distributed in the Republic of South Africa by:
Hay House SA (Pty), Ltd, PO Box 990, Witkoppen 2068.
Tel./Fax: (27) 11 467 8904. www.hayhouse.co.za

Published and distributed in India by:
Hay House Publishers India, Muskaan Complex, Plot No.3, B-2, Vasant Kunj, New
Delhi – 110 070. Tel.: (91) 11 4176 1620; Fax: (91) 11 4176 1630.
www.hayhouse.co.in

Distributed in Canada by:
Raincoast, 9050 Shaughnessy St, Vancouver, BC V6P 6E5.
Tel.: (1) 604 323 7100; Fax: (1) 604 323 2600

Text © Arielle Essex, 2013

A catalogue record for this book is available from the British Library.

ISBN 978-1-78180-075-1

Printed and bound in Great Britain by TJ International Ltd, Padstow, Cornwall

To all my clients who have taught me so much by opening their hearts and sharing their problems.

'Three things cannot be long hidden:
the sun, the moon, and the truth.'
Buddha

Contents

Contents

Contents

Acknowledgments

Throughout my journey, I've been very blessed to receive the support of many helpful, wise and generous people who have inspired me greatly. So my first thank you goes to all my teachers and guides who assisted my learning and healing. The concepts in this book represent my attempt to share some of the wisdom I've absorbed from all of them as well as the insights gained from working with clients.

I'd especially like to thank Michelle Pilley at Hay House for her belief in me and for encouraging me to write this book. I would also like to thank Sandy Draper and Julie Oughton as well as others who offered their time, insights, and expertise to help refine my message. I'm particularly grateful for the excellent feedback and advice given by Scott Ewing, Nicholas Pole, Anthony Williams, Alice Bergen, Suzanne Lovell, Dr. James Beattie, Anat Spitzer, Diana MacLellan, Jackie Pond, Saioa Velez, Anne Morgan, Eddie Solbrandt, and Peter Reynolds.

I'd also like to thank Karl Dawson, Harry Massey, Alexander Asseily, Simon Xavier Guerrand-Hermès, Kevin Laye, Eileen Campbell, Rose Hayman, Sue Head, Mervyn Lornie, Alan Pace, Lawrence Kershen, Anthony Bromousky, Jeremy Cassall, Helen Nicell, Brian Thorpe, Dr.

Satish Chandra, Gregg Becker, Rob Van Overburgen, Brian Van der Horst, and Carol Adrian Dermemgiu for all their encouragement and support.

The many sources of information, tools, and techniques are too numerous to list. However, for many of the concepts in this book I owe a special thank you to Paramahamsa Prajnananada Giri, Lynne McTaggart, Suzi Smith, Robert Dilts, Tim Halbom, Connirae Andreas, Michael Grinder, Anthony Robbins, Dr. Stephen Gilligan, Dr. Deepak Chopra, Dr. Bruce Lipton, Dr. Jerry Jampolsky, Louise Hay, Chuck Spezzano, Peter Fraser, HeartMath, IONS, and *A Course in Miracles*.

Foreword

You are holding *Practical Miracles* in your hands because, I imagine, it is an answer to a prayer. It is that sort of book. I trust that you are ready for some kind of miracle in your life because, I imagine, you wouldn't have dreamed of picking this book up if not. Therefore, what you have in your hands is not just a book; it's also both an opportunity and an invitation. This is your chance, and this is your moment, to heal your life.

Arielle Essex is the author of *Practical Miracles*. I first met Arielle 15 years ago, on a training program on psychology and spiritualty, held in central London. We were both students, and I remember how we enjoyed an instant connection that made me feel like we'd been friends forever. Arielle is that sort of person. Like all great teachers, Arielle is a great student. In *Practical Miracles* she presents a lifetime of learning that makes reading this book a truly healing experience.

In my work, I teach that people don't need more therapy, they need more clarity. Healing isn't about fixing someone who is broken; it's about restoring a memory of wholeness. The essence of who you are, your soul, remains unbroken; it's the ego (or self-image) that experiences fear and pain. Hence, the dark night of the soul is really a dark night of the ego. *Practical Miracles* helps you return to your real mind and to true consciousness.

Like Arielle, I am a student of *A Course in Miracles*. I love how Arielle skillfully presents major themes of this text, blending them together with timeless principles from Buddhism and Rumi, and also current thinking from NLP and coaching. I also love how Arielle shares intimately and honestly her own healing journey. Above all, this is what allows her to write *Practical Miracles* with such authority and clarity.

I love that *Practical Miracles* isn't that positive. As Arielle says, 'This book is not about positive thinking or shallow platitudes. It is not about blind faith or adopting a new spiritual belief. The shift of thinking required is no less than rediscovering the inner truth about who you really are.' Arielle doesn't want you to only be positive; she wants you to be honest and positive. It's when you are more honest with yourself than you have ever been that miracles occur.

Practical Miracles is rich with content. So much so, I imagine it will become a firm favourite with psychologists and healing practitioners. Arielle has been very generous in presenting so much great content in such a clear and concise way.

One last thought from me: please read this book slowly. Don't read it just to get to the end. It isn't that sort of book. *Practical Miracles* is a chance to slow down and to take direction from your real self. 'The miracle comes quietly into the mind that stops an instant and is still,' teaches *A Course in Miracles*. Here, in the stillness, is the memory of wholeness restored. Now the time for practical miracles begins.

I wish you well on your journey.

Robert Holden
Author of *Loveability* and *Shift Happens!*

Preface

'Love is the great miracle cure. Loving ourselves works miracles in our lives.'
Louise L. Hay

Thanks to information being so readily available, most of us are well aware of the value of positive thinking and natural healing. We're inspired by new scientific research explaining how everything works on the energetic and quantum level. We think we take good care of our health by following a good diet, taking vitamins, exercising regularly, meditating, and maybe following a spiritual path as well. According to statistics the majority of us have already experienced some form of complementary healing technique. Many readers may also have qualified in some form of therapy too. Before my personal healing journey began, this certainly described my life very well. So it was a big shock to be diagnosed with a brain tumor. The first thing it taught me was to have more humility about what I thought I knew.

Perhaps I had always been a slow learner. Despite my healing work and spiritual path, it seemed part of me remained so resistant to change and so unaware it was as if I was deaf and blind to my inner process. When I tell people my brain tumor healed without drugs or surgery it sounds impressive, until they hear that it took nearly 10 years. Who wants to spend 10 years getting well? Because the world moves so fast now, everyone expects instant results. Plus, truly miraculous healing stories abound: people who have had amazing spontaneous remissions in only days, weeks, or months!

For a long time hearing these stories made me feel nothing but frustrated and inadequate. After years of trying so hard, being so willing and doing everything I could, I didn't understand why a miracle hadn't happened for me. Why did my healing take so long? What had I overlooked? There must be some secret, some special strategy for making spontaneous remissions happen. With hindsight I saw that my long journey had given me a special bonus: I got to explore every obstacle that gets in the way. Of course no healing technique comes with a guarantee of success.

My heart grew full of compassion for those who share similar frustrations and possibly similar resistance too. Because my journey was so thorough, I hope sharing the insights I gained will provide useful stepping-stones for others. Having a clear path to follow makes it easier to navigate through challenging times. However, we need reasons before we make changes, or at least a reasonable understanding of why we should. A helpful guide can speed up the process. So for those who face a crisis, *Practical Miracles* is my attempt to offer a practical path.

The world now overflows with detailed information, transformative principles, effective techniques, healing gadgets, different remedies, alternative medicines, and intuitive insights. New scientific theories, in-depth research and amazing studies can now explain and verify why most of these work. Keeping up with everything becomes the new challenge. How can we decide what's best to do? My heart particularly goes out to those who feel desperate to find a solution that works. As one client said 'I've read all the books and spent a fortune going to seminars and workshops to learn zillions of magic-bullet techniques. How come they don't work for me? How come I'm still stuck?' There is always a good reason. Sometimes true kindness means facing difficult issues and saying what needs to be said. Understanding more about the different factors involved will help. Then it is possible to make better use of what we already know and the complexity starts to make more sense.

Thinking and stress

When my brain tumor was first diagnosed, my intuition told me that stress was the cause. However I had no idea where this stress had come from or why it affected my body in this particular way. The origin of my stress and what I could do about it was a mystery to be solved. Like a computer suffering a system overload, my brain worked overtime to process all the incoming data. This was my habitual pattern, trying so hard to make sense of things, and people had often told me that I was 'thinking too much.' As if I could somehow stop my brain racing from thought to thought! Of course, not only was that observation profoundly true but it also hinted at a possible solution. If only I had learned to master the power of my brain sooner!

Instead of learning how to direct my thinking, my head whirled with a cloud of unconscious thoughts swirling faster and faster, creating a tornado of stress. Not surprisingly I suffered terrible debilitating headaches often lasting for five days. Most of the time though, I remained oblivious of this inner turmoil. Like a swan gliding serenely on a pond, under the water of my calm exterior my feet were paddling like mad. I had the knack of looking superficially confident and together. Most of the time I succeeded in fooling myself too. Being a hard worker, I prided myself on being able to get things done and achieve most of my goals. Yet certain areas of my life were not going according to plan. Divorced, 39 years old, and desperately wanting to have a baby, I feared missing out on fulfilling my dreams. Years of disappointing relationships provided an obvious source of stress.

A phrase I often used to say was 'life is difficult.' Behind this little phrase lurked several unhelpful beliefs that needed to be shifted: why did I have to face so many difficult challenges? Why didn't my life go according to plan? Why did I suffer despite all my good behavior? The hidden expectation lurking behind these complaints was less obvious: life SHOULD be easy. Most people compare what they see on TV and in the movies with their life. It can seem like other people have it easy. But smart people know better than to make such comparisons. Instead they welcome their problems. After all, many people might have much worse! Facing a crisis calls for the courage to simply face 'the what is' and then find ways to resolve whatever needs to be healed.

Everything comes in threes

Several years before receiving the diagnosis of the brain tumor, a large cyst developed on my left ovary. The cyst had emerged during a particularly stressful relationship breakup. At the time it made perfect sense for my body to react to the emotional upset I felt. By coincidence I had arranged to visit a gifted healer who helped me release my upset and stress. To my delight the cyst magically dissolved and disappeared a few days later, just before my second ultrasound scan and scheduled surgery. Consequently, when the second scan showed everything looked normal, everyone concluded that it had been nothing important. Not surprisingly I made the mistake of believing the situation had resolved. I remained unaware of the underlying 'cloud' of stressful thoughts.

A few years later my extremely active prolactinoma was discovered during a routine checkup. Located in the pituitary, it was 1cm in diameter - the borderline size between malignant and benign. The extra cells were producing an excessive amount of prolactin hormone, 2,268mIU/L (normal range 250-400). Suddenly I was faced with barrage of scans, tests, visits to specialists, and many different recommendations. For the first year or two no one could confirm whether this tumor was malignant or benign. Luckily such tumors are not usually considered to be life-threatening. Even so the diagnosis felt shocking and there was a risk that the tumor could impinge on the optic nerve, causing loss of eyesight. Curiously both the ovarian cyst and the brain tumor produced the same side effect: infertility. The irony of this did not escape me! I wondered why my body wanted to prevent what I most wanted in life. It felt like internal sabotage.

Discovering what works

Of course I followed the advice of my doctors, did the recommended tests, had regular scans, and visited specialists. At that time there were only two medical treatments available for my tumor: surgery or a drug to slow down its growth.

Neither one promised effective nor long-term success. At the medical library I did my own research to find out as much as I could. The desire to heal my brain tumor greatly motivated my desire to learn. It comforted me to read that prolactinomas were very common and often only discovered on autopsy, and as many as two out of ten people might have one without ever knowing. Prolactinomas register high sensitivity to stress by increasing hormone production. So if I could reduce my stress levels, my regular blood tests would measure the level of hormones being produced and accurately indicate progress.

Because neither of the treatments promised much success, I chose to go down a different path and explore other options. I started learning neuro-linguistic programming (NLP), a practical psychological approach that emphasizes open-minded curiosity and the importance of keen observation. The theory and techniques I learned gave me deep insights and tools for reducing stress by changing beliefs, emotions, thoughts, and behaviors. NLP has helped many people heal all kinds of serious health problems and so I dedicated myself to learning and acquiring NLP expertise.

As I began to address the different aspects of my internal stress, my test results gave me regular feedback on what worked and what didn't. Although I still lacked clarity about what specific issues were linked to the tumor, resolving my problems led to feeling more at peace. However, when the tumor stubbornly stayed the same size for many years, pinpointing the precise cause became more important. What was I missing?

As my stress levels reduced, the activity of my tumor also diminished, so after three years my doctors labeled the tumor benign. This marked real progress. With the reduced risk of malignancy, there was less pressure to follow conventional treatment. So I had nothing to lose and everything to gain by continuing my inner healing process. I never gave up, despite occasional frustration. After my tumor finally healed without drugs or surgery, it took some time to unravel my long and complicated healing journey to establish what worked. Surprisingly it had little to do with physical body treatments; it had everything to do with learning how to bounce back from stress. The essence of what I had actually learned was how to deal with crisis, handle unconscious emotions, and develop resilience.

Later on I appreciated how the extra time made me become more thorough, developing deeper insights, acquiring more skill and getting more practice at directing my thoughts. My desire to heal made me persistently practice the techniques I learned and even do the exercises I read in books. Like a detective looking for clues, I paid attention to the seemingly insignificant thoughts, ideas and fantasies that flitted through my mind. I constantly looked for new ways to resolve seemingly unforgivable and impossible issues. Because I so often worked by myself, I also had to develop ways to double check whether I was kidding myself or not. Whenever I could, I sought the help of therapists for better objectivity, insights, assistance, and treatments. Although it was such a gift when people were there to act as my guides, pain and stress often occurred at times when no such help was available.

Refining the process

After my tumor healed, I wrote my first book *Compassionate Coaching* to describe the key elements of the process that worked for me, so that others could benefit too. Ironically my body then gave me yet another opportunity to test whether or not my process worked. Only a year or two after my brain tumor fully resolved, my breasts suddenly developed three highly active and aggressive lumps. Although I felt shocked and dismayed to face yet another diagnosis, it caused me much less stress. Staying calm, I applied my process with great curiosity to see whether or not it would work. The blessing of a physical issue is that symptoms offer clear measurements of whether or not progress is being made.

What I discovered was a deeper issue in my cloud of thoughts that I had not fully addressed. Owing to all my previous work, I found it easy to home in on the precise cause and work directly with this underlying issue. Using NLP and hypnosis, the resolution was quick. It took only one month to quiet down the inflammation around my breast lumps. By the time a biopsy was performed, the cells in the lumps were found to be benign. I preferred to trust the healing process of my body, and so I declined the recommended surgery. Without having any medical treatment, the lumps completely melted away over the next nine months and never returned. This happy result convinced me that the tools I will share with you in this book really can work.

After my healing story appeared in *The Living Matrix* documentary, many people told me how inspired they felt. Then they asked, 'But Arielle, how did you do that?' This made me realize that what seems obvious to me might not be so clear for everyone else to follow. Now after teaching these techniques, listening to clients, writing articles, and continuing my research for many years, I have been able to refine and clarify the essential elements. This book is my attempt to share the key elements of the processes that helped me.

Preface

There are much more impressive stories about amazing spontaneous remissions and miracle cures than mine. My doctors always assured me that my problems were nothing to worry about. In comparison with what other people suffer, they were minor problems. They were not life-threatening and could be expected to resolve with treatment. However the same could be said about the majority of complaints diagnosed. What makes my story worth sharing is how it motivated me to explore the links between conscious thoughts and stress and illness. For this reason I've used my story to highlight throughout the book some of the insights that helped me heal.

Having experienced my healings, as well as witnessing other people's astonishing recoveries, I'm convinced there are practical things we can do to encourage miraculous spontaneous remissions to occur more often. Healing begins by choosing to think differently. In a sense the real healing is the shift of thinking. We are all participating in an incredible wave of new information about science, energy, consciousness, and healing. We need to stretch the limits of what used to be thought possible. I hope this book assists you in bouncing back from any crisis to become a more resilient version of you. Please enjoy reinventing yourself and making the choices that heal.

Introduction

> '*The miracle is not to fly in the air, or walk on the water, but to walk on the Earth.*'
>
> **Chinese proverb**

Practical Miracles is about removing what blocks your natural healing power. By learning how to be free of old negative thinking, doubt and disbelief, we can become open-minded, connected and trust again. Blow away the old habitual thought clouds and develop a more loving, compassionate, healing attitude. This book is about consciousness: the mental and emotional aspects of healing. No one can fully explain consciousness. This could be why overlooking the conscious side of healing becomes the first problem to address.

Despite many studies confirming the effects of stress, confusion still clouds the issue of whether the mind and emotions really do affect the physical body. Lots of medics still choose to overlook any such connection and treat the body like a machine. The second problem is confusion about good versus bad stress: how much stress is okay; how good stress turns into bad stress; and exactly how stress translates into health problems. The third problem is the confusion between the conscious versus the unconscious mind. Although there may be no awareness of stress in the conscious mind, what lies in the unconscious mind remains hidden. Some people don't even believe they have an unconscious mind.

When faced with crisis, the temptation is to panic and rush into quick-fix solution mode. Getting immediate results becomes the focus. The confusion and overwhelm of facing a life-threatening diagnosis or some other huge challenge, leads to feeling lost and desperate. Very few know how to govern their emotions or focus their attention constructively. Very few remember to put their skills to good use or channel the power of thought. Stress clouds the conscious mind, making it difficult to think clearly. Unconscious habitual thinking takes over and creates a thick fog. Many blindly rush about trying new techniques, and give up too quickly when the latest magic pill doesn't produce the desired result.

Practical Miracles isn't offering a new magic-pill technique, nor is it about adopting a particular point of view: it is not about positive thinking or substituting belief for disbelief. It won't ask you to replace doubt with blind faith. It's normal to have doubts, but not helpful. Doubt means you may be looking for immediate results.

Each chapter addresses some of the common questions that clients often ask when they face a crisis. There is a logical sequence of exploration, discovery, and resolution. After practicing and mastering this strategy of thinking, it will become possible to do it quite quickly. Once you become aware of your inner 'thought clouds' and resolve the key issues, the less they will trouble you. You probably wouldn't be reading this book looking for answers unless some of the following common questions resonate with you:

‣ How can I make a miracle happen when I need one?

‣ How could this have happened to me, and why now?

‣ How is it possible that my thoughts have contributed to this?

‣ How can I resolve this problem and get rid of it right now?

‣ How is it possible to forgive what is unforgivable or let go?

‣ How can I bounce back and prevent it from happening again?

The answers to these questions and the choices described throughout this book will require intense self-honesty. Each chapter offers easy exercises to help you discover what you need to know. Reading the chapters in the right order might make more sense than skipping around. If you don't reach that place of inner peace and feeling better, it means you probably missed a piece or overlooked something. Sometimes the smallest items are the most vital steps of the process. Sometimes a particular choice needs to be addressed more fully and completely. If you have previously done lots of other therapy, be careful not to assume that you know everything without further exploration. Following the process thoroughly will work.

This path may not be for everyone

It has been my great privilege to witness many clients and students who have had the courage to face their problems and heal. Some of their stories have been used (with their permission) to illustrate how to follow the steps and embody the choices described in each section. Please remember that learning how to practice these skills must be done by choice, with total willingness, compassion, patience, and persistence.

Although much of this approach has been modeled from my healing success, I am not suggesting that the same will always work for everyone or that success is guaranteed. *Practical Miracles* is not a substitute for proper medical treatment. Please note that I always had medical doctors overseeing my process with proper assessments, lab tests, scans, etc. It's important to be responsible and get appropriate medical advice whenever you're facing a healing issue. Remember that medical interventions can be vehicles to assist the natural Grace of healing, too.

Despite whatever expertise and prior therapeutic training we have, it is also highly advisable to seek good therapists and coaches to assist during a healing journey. Stuck thinking prevents progress. It can be very difficult to be objective or insightful about our familiar ways of thinking. Habitual thoughts always sound sensible, true and beyond question. They often preclude being able to see clearly. We can save ourselves lots of time by working with a good guide who can listen between the words and challenge these ideas.

Learning to apply these principles and make these choices will not interfere with other treatments. In fact *Practical Miracles* should enhance and enrich the success of other approaches. The body is capable of incredible self-healing. Over a third of most illnesses will resolve with or without medical intervention. Placebos work as well as many drugs. The thoughts we choose are more important than which treatments we choose. What we believe, what we decide, and what we feel passionate about has the most profound effect.

This book is for those who face big challenges, who are highly aware, intelligent, and may already have experience or know some good techniques. *Practical Miracles* will show you how to apply your skills more effectively and when to use techniques and tools for best results. When the approach being used hasn't worked, perhaps there could be a deeper aspect to explore. Stress can leave you shell-shocked, exhausted, and so weary that nothing makes sense anymore. The cure is to reconnect with your essence, rediscover what makes you unique, and recommit to giving your gifts.

Spontaneous remissions

In 2009 Lynne McTaggart's wonderful journal *What Doctors Don't Tell You* published a fascinating article about the research undertaken by 'The Institute for Noetic Science' (IONS) in California. IONS studied what helped 1,574 people to have medically documented, spontaneous remissions from cancer. What's amazing is that all these people made the same eight mental and emotional changes. This information may provide a very useful checklist to guide you on your healing journey:

1. A shift from dependency to autonomy combined with activities, attitudes and behaviors that promote increased autonomy and increased awareness of themselves, of others and their environment, and also increased love, joy, playfulness, satisfaction, laughter and humor.

2. Facing the crisis and having the power to find a new way of life that is fulfilling and meaningful.

3. Taking control of their lives, including personal, professional, emotional, spiritual and medical aspects, and reappraising old beliefs that are no longer appropriate or adequate.

4. Becoming comfortable with and expressing positive and negative emotions, and finding the ability to say 'no' when necessary for their wellbeing.

5. Having at least one strong loving relationship, and a connection with an organization.

6. Working in partnership with their physician.

7. Finding meaning in the experience of cancer, finding reasons to live and accepting the diagnosis – but not the prognosis – of cancer, and believing in a positive outcome.

8. Choosing activities that promote awareness and reduce stress, and showing renewed spiritual awareness that can lead to a spiritual practice such as prayer or meditation.[1]

Most of these points could also be adapted and applied to any type of crisis. They provide good advice for us to follow at any time. Satisfying each of these different elements may provide good preventative medicine too. What worked for these people should work for everyone. Throughout this book each chapter will offer insights into satisfying these factors through helpful explanations and specific exercises.

Acid test questions

As a way to check whether or not each step has been completed before moving on to the next one, there are special test questions provided and labeled 'Acid Test Question.' An antique expert tests the genuine quality of fine silver by using a drop of nitric acid to assess what percentage of pure silver is in the metal object. So, metaphorically speaking, these questions provide measurements to determine whether you have genuinely completed and fulfilled each step. When doing exercises by yourself, it can be so easy to overlook habitual stuck thinking. The purpose of these checks is to prevent any tendency to kid yourself or possibly miss important opportunities for change. Here's the first one.

ACID TEST QUESTION
How will you know the Practical Miracles process is working?

The short-term benefits are immediate: expect more clarity, calmness, deeper understanding, and a feeling of being centered, lighter, and relaxed. From this place you will find it easier to be proactive, motivated, persistent, and determined. Internal stress levels should quiet down, leaving your body free to heal. You may notice you react to events differently. Decisions and choices become easier to make. You may become more curious and observant, noticing how events reflect your thinking patterns. Internal mind chatter quiets down. You may begin to notice improvements in physical, emotional or mental ability, as well as relationships. Old events from the past no longer bother you.

At the end of each chapter you will find some 'Key points' to review what you've just read. There are also a few 'Choice Thoughts' to meditate on or use as prayers. If you use EFT (emotional freedom technique) you might find these useful to tap on. In the middle of a crisis, reading a book may require too much energy and concentration. So these gentle reminders might come in handy then, too.

Long-term benefits depend on how well you continue to practice and maintain the positive changes you make. Your energy, passion, and creativity should continue to increase. People often report that they feel they 'get their life back.' There is no problem that cannot be healed. Somewhere on the planet, someone has faced the same issue and healed it. If it is possible for one person to do something, then it must be possible for others, too. If you have tried everything else and nothing has worked, then you have nothing to lose. The only side effect will be a deeper level of understanding. *Practical Miracles* may help you put your finger on the precise point that you missed before.

My hope is that each exercise will provide you with the opportunity to test these ideas for yourself. Making your own discoveries is what counts. Shifting your thoughts will be the real measure of your progress. What is right for you, what you accept, what you choose, all express your uniqueness. Healing is about restoring your wholeness. Nothing can help you find peace but yourself. It is not about the length of life, but the quality of life. My wish is for you to reconnect and remember who you are, to forgive what's past and to look forward with joy and positive expectancy.

'Do not believe in anything simply because you have heard it. Do not believe in anything simply because it is spoken and rumored by many. Do not believe in anything simply because it is found written in your religious books. Do not believe in anything merely

on the authority of your teachers and elders. Do not believe in traditions because they have been handed down for many generations. But after observation and analysis, when you find that anything agrees with reason and is conducive to the good and benefit of one and all, then accept it and live up to it.'

Buddha

Chapter 1

How Can You Make a Miracle Happen When You Need One?

What you are about to read will change your life forever! At last you can learn the secret that has never been revealed before. You can be one of the first to rediscover the ancient knowledge that has been hidden for centuries. This amazing magic will heal everything, cure everything, and fix your whole life instantly - no effort required! It's fast, effective, long lasting, and FREE! At last you will be able to solve those problems that have kept you stuck for so long.

Here's the question: did reading that first paragraph pique your interest? Did you feel your hope and energy rise? Did a part of your mind get curious to read further? Or perhaps you felt a twinge of skepticism as you said to yourself: 'Haven't I heard this somewhere before?' Maybe you felt completely cynical and switched off. Notice what sort of response went through your mind. How often do you get bombarded by offers, adverts, invitations, products, or promises that make outrageous claims for amazing benefits?

No matter how many times we may have heard approaches like that, such promises may still push our buttons and hook our interest. Of course some do it better than others. Marketing depends on understanding how people's minds work. What makes people think the way they think? What drives people to do the things they do? What causes illness and what helps healing? People who want to heal a problem or an illness often seek 'the magic pill.' They secretly hope to find something to take away the problem quickly. What they really want is to resume living exactly as they did before.

> *'If you believe everything you read, better not read.'*
> Japanese proverb

Miracles do happen. To learn how to create a *Practical Miracle* we need to understand how the mind works and how thoughts affect healing. There are many different factors involved in the creation and resolution of a health issue. This book will focus on how to assist your body's natural healing by reducing stress through changing your thinking. Although different healing approaches help at different levels, dealing with this aspect of consciousness will accelerate the effectiveness of whatever treatments you choose. The word 'healing' comes from an old Germanic root *hælan*, which means 'to make whole, sound, and well.' Wholeness means to be consciously one with everything. So this gives a clue about the process explained in this book.

According to biologist Dr. Bruce Lipton, 80 percent of illnesses will heal with or without any treatment. A mere 10 percent of illness is actually helped by medical intervention. Placebos effectively score between 33 percent and 75 percent success, even when people know they are receiving placebos. Drugs barely outperform placebos in drug trials. Plus, the placebo effect of receiving a drug from a doctor in a hospital setting is overlooked. Do people get better from the treatment or from their belief in the treatment? The power of placebos can no longer be ignored. Instead, the powerful source of healing within the mind that believes in the placebo should be investigated more deeply[1].

Of course it would be irresponsible not to seek medical advice and follow appropriate treatment whenever necessary. When you need to heal, it makes sense to do everything you can to assist your body and mind to get back into balance. If a doctor prescribes a course of treatment, it makes no sense to take one dose and then stop because you don't get an immediate result. You need to take the whole course of treatment and give the body time to recover. The same principle applies to working with the mind. You need to continue making necessary changes until a lasting perceptible shift has occurred. *Practical Miracles* are not meant to be a substitute for following appropriate medical advice; the aim is to supplement your chosen healing path and make it more effective.

Facing a crisis

In this curious world it appears that things just happen. It seems like we have little control over events. However, whether or not we can control events, we can control how we respond. When life sails along smoothly and everything is going our way, feeling happy is easy. Floating on good luck and good fortune, we get lulled into thinking that such carefree moments will last forever. But the river of life never runs without twists and turns and surprises. Placid friendly water changes fast in stormy weather. A sudden crisis creates shock and upset. Tidal waves may rock the beliefs that form our comfort zones.

If you perceive yourself to be a victim of events beyond your control, you simultaneously become disempowered and somewhat helpless. Your choices are instantly limited. Perhaps you've already hit some rough water. When life doesn't go according to plan, when problems loom, or when you've received a shocking diagnosis, it is time to learn how to weather the storm. Facing a crisis demands different choices.

Coping with disruptive change requires developing real resilience. This means having the certainty of knowing you can recover from misfortune and weather any form of adversity. You need a strong, robust, and resilient body: resilience in making decisions and choices, as well as a resilient attitude of thinking. Your body is reflected in the mirror. Your character is reflected in your decisions, choices, and actions. Your attitude, thoughts, and beliefs are reflected in your results. When you need different results, when you need to heal your body, mind, or emotions you are being called to think differently. As soon as you change your thinking, your emotions will follow suit. If you want happiness and peace, choose to think differently. This book will help you identify which thoughts need to be reconsidered so you can find that inner calm. Once your mind no longer feels stressed, your body can get on with the natural process of healing.

> '*In the confrontation between the stream*
> *and the rock, the stream always wins – not*
> *through strength, but through persistence.*'
> Buddha

When faced with crisis people need answers fast, they want help, and they don't know what to do. It is quite normal to hope for miracles and wish the crisis would disappear. Life is busy enough without extra problems to deal with: it is logical to want a quick solution in order to get on with life as usual; it isn't good news to hear that health issues might be related to problems that haven't yet been solved. Therefore at the beginning of a healing journey, as mentioned earlier, the questions most commonly asked sound like:

- How can I make a miracle happen when I need one?
- How could this have happened to me, and why now?
- How is it possible that my thoughts have contributed to this?
- How can I resolve this problem and get rid of it right now?
- How is it possible to forgive what is unforgivable or let go?
- How can I bounce back and prevent it from happening again?

In order to heal or resolve any crisis there's no need to turn yourself into a self-improvement project. A complete overhaul is not necessary. Just learn how to make the kind of choices that heal. Whatever has motivated you to read this book, whatever problems you might need to resolve, remember you are already perfect the way you are. Being alive means your purpose has not been completed yet. So that means there is still time for growth, evolution, and positive change! A problem you currently face merely invites you to make some specific change so that your life can become more meaningful, happy, and peaceful. This book seeks to help remove the obstacles.

What is a miracle?

According to the dictionary, a miracle is 'a marvelous event manifesting a supernatural act contrary to established laws of nature and attributed to a Divine cause.' The word comes from the Latin *miraculum,* which means 'object of wonder' and its ultimate root meant 'to smile upon.' What would it take for you to smile upon your problems?

A different definition comes from the insightful metaphysical book, *A Course in Miracles,* which says 'a miracle is a shift in perception.' Therefore a *Practical Miracle* involves shifting the perception and choosing practical thoughts in order to enhance healing and build resilience. Insights from *A Course in Miracles* inspired me greatly on my healing journey, so I've included several quotes throughout the book to share some of this timeless wisdom; its principles help to reveal many of the thoughts and belief patterns that can prevent progress. After identifying a thought that needs to be changed, it then becomes a simple matter of choosing how to think differently. Shifting to more practical and more loving thoughts lowers stress levels and consequently assists healing.

Facing a serious problem means it is time to get practical. First it requires facing the issue, and dealing with the crisis as best you can. Avoid going into denial and pretending you are okay. Instead honestly assess the situation and make whatever adjustments necessary in order to feel physically, mentally, and emotionally comfortable. Then address the deeper levels of thought and belief. *Practical Miracles* require you to make some specific shift in thinking. You don't have to change your entire belief system. This book is not about positive thinking or shallow platitudes. It is not about blind faith or adopting a new spiritual belief. The shift of thinking required is no less than rediscovering the inner truth about who you really are. This book is for all the people who have asked, 'but how do you do that?'

> '*I have seen a medicine that's*
> *able to breathe life into a stone.*'
> William Shakespeare, *All's Well That Ends Well*

The fix-it approach of healing the physical symptoms of a problem may be necessary and helpful, but may not result in complete transformation. Doing the right things like good diet, exercise, rest, appropriate treatment, etc., demonstrate great commitment in taking care of yourself. Unfortunately, you can be doing all the right physical things and still experience problems. Remember that even spiritual gurus suffer illnesses and pass away. Conversely there are many people who have suffered severe illness, had near-death experiences, and then fully recovered. It may be of interest to note that these people who enjoy spontaneous remissions usually shift their thinking so intensely that their whole lives change in the process.

Confusion about stress

Stress gets a lot of bad press. Most people talk about being stressed as a negative state. But who would want a life completely devoid of challenge? Although it sounds desirable to aim for peace, harmony and happiness, a steady diet of nothing but bliss might feel a bit bland. Positive stress motivates you to do more, try harder, meet the challenge, and win! No one likes being bored, so perhaps having problems is a way to make life more interesting. However having too many problems crosses a threshold and tips your life into unhealthy stress, feeling overwhelmed, and exhausted. The trick must be to keep the amount of stress in balance.

....

Most of the things that cause stress occur outside of conscious awareness: for example, a little healthy competition, pushing yourself to achieve a new target, taking on a big job, stretching yourself to learn something new, making changes in daily life, moving house, starting a relationship. Whenever a new activity begins to require more of your attention, care and decision-making, you feel more alive, more aware, and conscious. As long as all goes well, it feels exciting. Although it takes effort, you meet the challenges, achieve the targets, and succeed at your objectives. You are still within your comfort zone, feeling motivated and excited.

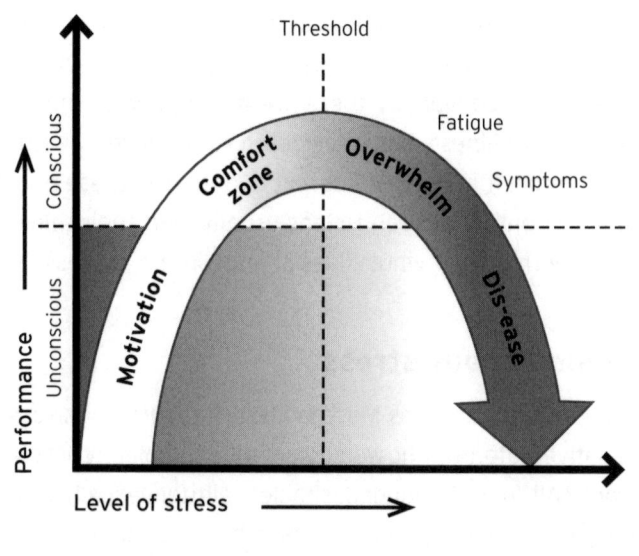

The stress threshold

If the challenges continue too long, or the mounting stack of stressful problems grows too high, or the deadlines can't be met, or the number of unfinished jobs feels unfulfilling, then you pass the threshold from good to bad stress. Instead of feeling energized, motivated, and excited by the challenges, you feel fatigue, exhaustion, and burnout. Because stress hormones keep the body in emergency mode, the immune system can't function well. Over time, this kind of grinding stress builds up in the body, causing symptoms and dis-ease.

> '*A hero is one who knows how to*
> *hang on one minute longer.*'
> Norwegian proverb

EXERCISE
How much stress is good for you?

Here is a quick and easy way to assess your level of stress. Just check out your current state and give yourself a score 0–10 for each of descriptions below. Add up your scores for each column and notice which column receives the highest score. A healthy level of stress feels energized, exciting, and motivated. Warning levels indicate it's time to reassess the situation and make some changes.

Healthy stress	Score	Warning levels of stress	Score
High energy		Low energy, tired, burned-out	
Sleeping soundly, long		Sleeping poorly, not enough	
Healthy immune system		Symptoms, illness, disease	
Clear thinking		Confused, making mistakes	
Normal blood pressure		High blood pressure	
Normal cholesterol		Raised cholesterol	
Good skin, hair, nails		Problems with skin, hair, nails	
Feeling calm, at peace		Weepy, grouchy, moody	

Warning levels of stress mean it is time to take positive action before the body begins to suffer. Stress is now accepted as a major factor, if not the cause, of illness. The dis-ease process begins when negative emotions accumulate due to thoughts repeatedly looping in the mind. The body starts reacting to the negative thoughts and emotions and stops functioning normally. Negative thoughts and emotions form traffic jams in the neural pathways, diminishing the delivery of messages to specific organs. Even small amounts of dis-ease, the little worrying thoughts that get repeated on a daily basis, can add up to chronic stress conditions. Stress creates tension, tightness, and restriction. Negative thinking is toxic. Every thought and every feeling radiates waves of energy that register in the body. However, an idle passing thought has less effect than repetitive thoughts chattering away in the mind with lots of emotion.

The stress spiral

The body registers all stress whether we are consciously aware of it or not. Stressful feelings that are not addressed and resolved get suppressed into the body. The following diagram supplies a simple explanation of the process of how the 'adrenal stress response' is triggered. Each time an event triggers a stressful thought the result is an associated negative feeling. The type of feeling depends on the underlying needs associated with those thoughts. It doesn't matter whether the thought gets expressed or suppressed. At some point the unconscious mind 'checks' whether or not the underlying needs are satisfied or not: 'Yes' or 'No.' When the needs get met, the feelings subside and peace returns to an okay state. If the needs don't get met then the feelings activate hormones causing the adrenal stress response, which has repercussions throughout the body. The stress continues to spiral around the same circuit again, increasing in volume each time if it isn't resolved.

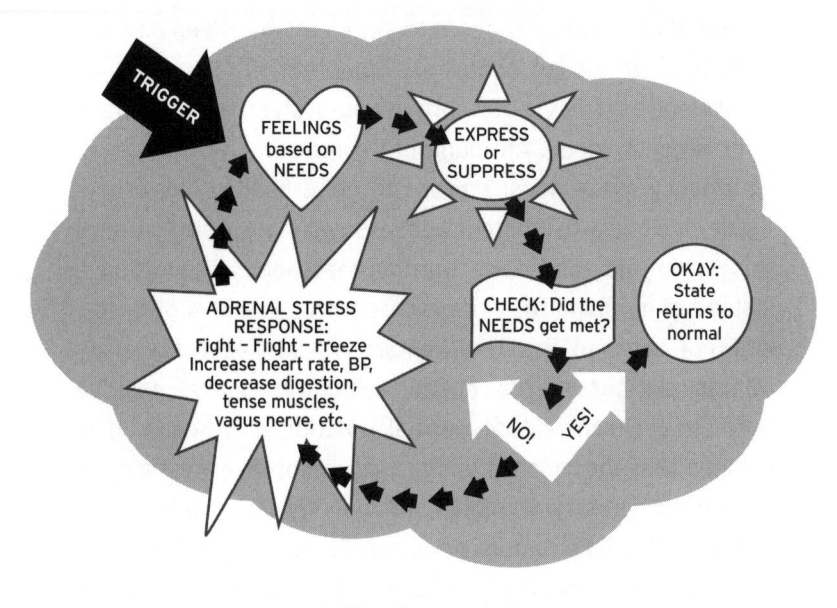

The stress spiral

With each spiral, the hypothalamus and limbic system amplify the adrenal stress response affecting organs, glands, and tissues throughout the body. Muscles tense, joints stiffen, heart rate and blood pressure go up, and the vagus nerve slows down all the less essential body processes (e.g. the immune response and digestion). Energy diverts to what is commonly known as the 'fight or flight' adrenal stress response: the body prepares to stand and fight or to run away. After careful observation of how different people react to stress, it is more accurate to expand this to the 'four Fs response': fight, flight, freeze, or fall asleep. The 'freeze' response is behaving like a startled rabbit caught in a car's headlights. Neither running away nor fighting, this describes how someone gets frozen into non-action. The 'fall asleep' response resembles the way a mouse plays dead when caught by a cat. Stress can build up so high that the body chooses to switch off and sleep day and night to try to escape, almost like hibernating.

As long as stress spirals through the system, the body stays in emergency mode. Although not completely dysfunctional, emergency mode doesn't promote good health. Any organ, tissue, or gland with inherent weakness will start to suffer under this strain and send early warning messages as symptoms. Instead of numbing these messages with painkillers or drugs, why not learn to listen? When we are at peace the body relaxes and our internal chemical factory releases positive hormones, which restore normal function and health. It is obvious that the most effective way to improve wellbeing is to shift our stressful thoughts and feelings. Positive thoughts and emotions help restore natural balance. This book aims to help you make the mental and emotional changes that will enhance this positive healing power.

The fix-it model

The fix-it-mechanical model treats the body like a car that has been vandalized or attacked by dis-ease functions, bacteria, or viruses running out of control. Specialists jump to the rescue in full emergency mode, replacing parts and stifling the symptoms with drugs. Elaborate tests, Latin labels, scientific reasons, complex explanations, and theories absorb all the attention and complicate the issue. No one pays much attention to the real cause of the problem. The focus is to get rid of the symptoms instead of listening to them as messages and clues. No one pays attention to who is driving the car!

All thoughts create waves of energy that radiate and resonate with the energy all around you. Just as positive thoughts have incredible healing power, there must be negative thoughts at the root of stress and the source of disease. No one gets up in the morning and decides to have a major crisis, grow a tumor, or catch a cold. But what if a part of you did choose what has happened? This isn't to suggest that you *consciously* chose the challenges you face. No one does that. However few people have awareness of the thoughts lurking in their unconscious mind. Don't blame yourself for the problems you face or you'll double how bad you feel in an instant. Feeling guilty serves no good purpose. Taking responsibility, however, doesn't mean taking the blame.

During my healing journey, what held me back for many years was my total refusal to believe that any part of me had chosen to create my tumor. Because I was so totally focused on my consciously held goals, I remained totally unaware that another part of me was moving in the opposite direction. With hindsight that sounds rather strange. Surely my tumor didn't jump into my head from outer space. So who could have created the stressful energy that aggravated my condition if it wasn't me?

People often treat their cars better than their bodies. An expensive sports car gets cleaned, polished, filled with the best fuel, and serviced regularly. How many people treat their bodies with the same high-quality attention? How many pay attention to the quality of the food they feed themselves, or how much exercise and rest their body needs? Instead of valuing their health, they take it for granted. Later, when the body starts to malfunction, they feel surprised.

Newtonian physics provided a basis for explaining the universe as mechanical. This scientific understanding led to thinking that the body operates like a machine; therefore health problems need to be fixed by chemicals, drugs, or surgery. However quantum physics is proving that the invisible, immaterial realm of energy is far more important than the physical world of matter. This new science offers challenging new ideas about how the energy of thoughts shapes not only the body but also the environment.

In the West we still tend to view the body as separate from the mind and emotions. This idea gets amplified when treatments assault the body with brutal interventions instead of restoring the natural balance between body and mind. Plus most insurance companies work on the basis that the patient is a victim of random misfortune. Would they be so willing to fund treatment if the patient owned responsibility for the cause? In addition most research supports the current medical model by hunting for guilty viruses, genes, malfunction, and broken parts. Perhaps the amazing developments they achieve might work even better if the basic premise focused more on reactivating the natural healing of the body.

Thanks to recent scientific discoveries and the new understanding about quantum physics and energy, most people are now much more aware. They realize the limitations of current medical thinking and ask more questions. Oddly enough hospitals and medical schools use sophisticated diagnostic equipment, which depends on technology based on quantum theory, yet they haven't incorporated the significance of energy and quantum mechanics into the medical approach. It is possible to read more about the amazing healing ability of the body's energy system, atomic structure, and the quantum field in many books, articles, and blogs as well as YouTube videos, but fully comprehending these new concepts isn't essential for using the processes described in this book. If you would like to know more, please see the list of recommended reading at the back of the book. Rather than discuss theories of quantum physics, this book will specifically focus on how to change your thinking in order to accelerate healing.

Taking responsibility means being practical and pragmatic

Of course the body does need good care and appropriate treatment. Emergency interventions can save lives and buy valuable time. Making the best use of the medical science available just makes good sense. However, facing the vast array of tests and treatments being offered can feel overwhelming. How do you know how to make the right choice?

The best way to make a good decision is to ask yourself what you truly believe will help. Avoid being pushed into following procedures by well-meaning helpers. Where you put your confidence, where you put your trust, and what you believe will work all enhance the effectiveness of whatever medicine you choose. Lots of placebo studies have proved that belief is more important than what is in the medicine. For example, a recent and well-documented study published in the New England Journal of Medicine describes a report on 180 patients who required knee surgery for osteoarthritis. The patients were divided into three groups and told they were part of a study where some of them would only receive placebo surgery. During the study, one group received proper surgery to remove torn cartilage, the second group merely had the cartilage flushed out, and the third group underwent simulated arthroscopic surgery, the placebo in which an incision was made and sewn up, but nothing was removed.[3]

During the two-year follow-up, patients in all three groups reported moderate improvement in both pain reduction and function. Surprisingly the placebo patients often reported better outcomes. One man who received only the placebo surgery, refused to believe he had *not* received the actual surgery because his pain had vanished and his movement had improved so greatly.

There are no guarantees with any treatment, or with the processes recommended in this book. However, when we discover new understandings and begin to feel more at peace, stress levels reduce. When we feel more able to give our love freely as a result of following the processes, such as the ones outlined in this book, surely that's the important part of healing. It's not just about removing the symptoms.

> 'The greatest discovery of my generation is that human beings can alter their lives by altering their attitude of mind. If you change your mind, you can change your life.'
> William James

Having worked for many years in the field of complementary medicine, I had more trust in my body's natural healing power than in medical treatment. However after six months of dealing with having a tumor and amplifying the stress by having scans, tests and seeing many specialists, my resolve wore thin. Then a funny thing happened when I actually considered undergoing surgery to remove the tumor. I became very aware of my prejudice against medical interventions! It made me smile to realize how this was the perfect mirror opposite to the prejudice many medical practitioners feel about alternative treatments.

At the medical library I researched the facts and discovered the surgery recommended for my tumor had a low success rate: 50 percent of the tumors grew back after the operation. Even so, I decided my prejudice was limiting and not helpful. After all, many people undergo surgery and heal. Couldn't the Grace of healing come through any type of well-intentioned treatment? So I decided to let go of my prejudice and sought the advice of the recommended neurosurgeon. I entered his office totally willing to undergo surgery. However after carefully viewing my MRI scans, the surgeon declared that my tumor was inoperable due to its location. Surprised and relieved, I walked out of his office with a huge smile on my face! This meant I now had no choice but to find a way to heal the tumor myself.

Being too attached to the outcome

Do you feel so attached to the idea of immediately getting rid of your problem that anything less than that sounds disappointing? Does the desire to heal drive you to chase every magic pill technique promising a quick fix? It may be compelling to think you are actively pursuing your goal, but you could end up running around in circles. Being too attached to getting results means too limited a focus and too little flexibility. The quality of your life, how you spend your time and energy, how you show up, and how you want to be remembered may be more important than the particular result you chase. Every good moment, every bad moment, and every aspect of the journey is precious.

Some people worry that if they take responsibility for creating their problem they will receive less sympathy and help. Unfortunately being a victim and being cared for leads to a possible trap. Both the victim and the helper become ensnared in a complicity that leaves little room for change. Some people believe that if they assumed responsibility, they wouldn't deserve assistance. The illness may have become a strategy for getting other needs met. Of course accepting full responsibility could have the opposite effect. People might think more highly of you. What if people were so inspired by your courage and authenticity in being responsible that they wanted to help you more?

Putting a label on the illness also makes it seem too concrete. The named illness becomes a nominalization, a set thing. Having an illness is such a big story that it becomes an identity. Saying 'I'm a cancer victim' is not helpful. Whatever is happening in the body is a process, not something solid. Nothing has been written in stone. Scary medical labels keep people locked in a stuck version of reality. It is much better to turn any such labels back into actions, which sound like flexible behaviors. For example, turn cancer into 'cancer-ing,' or hypertension could become 'hyper-tensing.' Then it sounds more possible to stop doing that behavior. When you turn it back into an action, it seems easier to reverse the process. For example, what I said to myself was that my body just liked 'making lumps.' That sounded less scary than having a tumor and it gave me the choice to stop making lumps and do something different.

ACID TEST QUESTION
How responsible do you feel and how well do you meet your unconscious needs?

First score how much you think you're <u>not</u> to blame for what is currently happening in your life: 0–100. That's how much you feel like a victim. Subtract that score from 100. The remainder is the percentage of responsibility and power you are willing to accept right now. The quickest way to tell if your needs are being met is to gauge how you feel. When needs have been met there will be peace, happiness, and satisfaction. When they are not, there will be negative feelings: disappointment, irritation, annoyance, agitation, anxiety, etc. So having negative feelings means it is time to find out what those unmet needs might be. (Remember the 'Acid Test Questions' are to help you check that you've fulfilled each step before going on to the next.)

Facing a crisis of any kind is a wake-up call in disguise. Think of it as an unexpected opportunity to help you learn and grow in ways you never thought possible. In this fast-paced, chaotic world ample opportunities of all shapes and sizes come your way to test you. How you choose to meet those challenges determines your success and reveals your character and true nature. What if you believed that you're never given more than you can handle? Then facing enormous challenges would mean you must have enormous capabilities! Perhaps having a big problem just means you are an ambitious soul.

Stress both challenges and stretches you to the limits of your capabilities. How willing are you to address your feelings and change your thoughts? What happened in the past does not have to determine the future. Worrying, feeling overwhelmed, angry, fearful, guilty, or depressed indicates the presence of old thinking that needs to change. When you face a serious crisis or dis-ease there is no time to waste. If you don't know what to do, some of the ideas in this book will help. Clinging to what you already know and repeating old habits won't work. Be willing to ask yourself some new questions and find some new answers. Choose to think again, think with love, and think more wisely.

> *'There is no journey, but only an awakening.'*
> *A Course in Miracles*, Anon

Developing resilience

Once we manage to get through a crisis there is often the worry that it could happen again. We want long-lasting resilience to give us the confidence to know we can handle any future stress. The word resilience comes from the Latin *resilire*, which means to 'spring back, rebound, and recover from being stretched.' Wouldn't we like to be able to bounce back from setbacks, sustain our energy under constant pressure and meet the challenges of life with acceptance and a smile? What if problems could be viewed as positive motivation toward change and growth? This book will show how to develop this buoyant kind of resilience, by first letting go of what no longer works and then being flexible enough to make specific changes in our thinking.

Wishing something would happen will not make it happen. Resisting change won't stop change from occurring.

Maintaining the status quo just keeps us stuck in the same place. Avoid creating an identity around suffering. When people say things like, 'I'm afraid to change because then I wouldn't be me' or 'It's just not the right time, I don't know enough yet, I need to feel certain.' That is just fear doing the talking.

When a river hits boulders in its path, the water flows around and over them. In time the water wears those rocks away, leaving them smooth and rounded. Learning how to make better choices helps the river of life flow more smoothly, no matter what the terrain. The more we try to hold on to old ways, resisting the force of the river, the more we amplify the problem. The more responsibility we accept for the current situation, the more empowered we become to change things. Miracles begin with a change of thinking; so making a miracle happen is that easy.

Key points

▶ To create a *Practical Miracle* you need to understand how the mind works and how thoughts affect healing.

▶ When your mind is no longer stressed, your body can get on with healing.

▶ It is essential to face the issue and deal with the crisis.

▶ Positive stress is motivating, challenging, and makes life interesting.

▶ Unhealthy stress leads to fatigue, exhaustion, and dis-ease.

▶ Stress triggers the adrenal stress response: fight, flight, freeze, or fall asleep.

- Resilience means being able to bounce back from setbacks, sustain your energy under constant pressure, and meet the challenges of life with acceptance and a smile.

- The more responsibility you accept for the current situation, the more empowered you become to change things.

··

Choice Thoughts

This problem invites me to think differently.

I am never given more than I can handle.

Positive stress motivates me and makes life interesting.

Resisting change will not stop change from occurring.

A big problem means I am ambitious for growth.

I am open to asking questions and finding new answers.

I have the power to govern my thoughts and emotions.

Chapter 2

Mental Medicine: Healing the Heart of the Mind

No matter what the problem, or how big the crisis, is it possible to accept that for some reason things have to be this way, at this particular moment? Instead of wasting time and energy resisting, blaming, thinking it's an accident outside of our control, believing it's bad luck, fate, or God's punishment, just be curious about how things could unfold in a better way. Being grateful for what we still have frees us to make better choices and set new outcomes. What is the best choice we could make right now? Take the responsibility to picture how things could turn out for the better. Accept whatever has happened. A good question to ask is: 'What do I have right now, and what can I do with that?' Responsibility starts with acceptance.

Choose your response

No matter what has occurred, we always have a choice about how we respond. What we think and feel is totally under our control if we learn how to direct the power of our own mind. Accepting responsibility means choosing to respond intelligently. We need to take charge of our minds and emotions and make decisions that align with what is most important. Being responsible requires being curious enough to explore our unconscious thoughts and beliefs. The act of accepting responsibility puts us firmly in the driving seat. The more responsibility we assume, the more power we have to change. If our thoughts and beliefs have created something we don't like, then we can un-create it by thinking differently. Instead of being a victim, our journey becomes an adventure of discovering new ways to respond.

At first, when facing my predicament, I found it hard to believe I had anything to do with creating my tumor. Why do bad things happen to good people? Despite doing all the right things, my good behavior was not being rewarded! Despite knowledge of the mind-body connection, I couldn't understand what I had done wrong or how I had anything to do with the process. I blamed my body for sabotaging my best plans for the future. I wondered if I was the victim of a curse, or bad astrological configurations, or whether I was being punished. This line of thinking didn't work very well for me. It was a waste of time and energy. There has to be a better choice.

There's a spiritual principle that maintains we would not be able to see negative things in the world unless they already exist somewhere within our mind. The degree to which we must move away from what we judge as negative equals the degree to which we fear we could be like that ourselves. The greater the judgment and condemnation, the greater the energy involved. Even though this negative energy is outside of awareness, it must find an outlet. So typically the energy gets suppressed into the body. Although good people would never dream of hurting anyone else, they unwittingly end up hurting themselves. These unconscious thoughts lodge in some part of the body creating tension, inflicting pain or causing other problems.

'There is no such thing as an idle thought.
Every miracle is preceded by a change in thinking.
All thoughts create form on some level.
Every thought leads either to Love or Fear.'
A Course in Miracles, Anon

Identity and immunity

Bacteria, viruses, and cancer cells don't thrive unless they find the right environment that welcomes them. Foreign invaders can't jump into the body and take over without being given full room and board. In a healthy body bacteria, viruses, and cancer cells get removed daily as part of the body's natural ecological defense. Our immune system's white blood cells constantly scan our bodies for anything that doesn't belong. Whenever something looks suspicious, the white blood cells have to determine whether to remove the unwelcome alien or allow it to take up residence.

How can the immune system do this job properly without a clear sense of your identity? If you don't know who you are, how can your white blood cells decide what belongs inside you and what does not? If there's a lack of clarity, then it's easy to understand why the white blood cells sometimes make mistakes. If alien invaders aren't recognized, the white blood cells may fail to stop them before they multiply and cause problems. If your own body cells aren't recognized, the white blood cells may attack them by mistake, causing autoimmune problems. Many things can interfere with the immune system's natural healthy balance. The job is to discover what has interfered with yours.

Most people think they know who they are. Privately they may admit that their sense of identity is a by-product of the roles they perform: teacher, coach, or some other job description – mother, father, wife, husband, friend, etc. Beyond these sorts of roles how would you define yourself? Maybe you've heard the old cliché about people who say they are human beings but live their lives as if they are human doings. Their worth and sense of self depend on what they do, how well they do it, and how much they achieve or acquire. They have little awareness about their true identity. The confusion begins with all the influences that contribute to this limited sense of self such as family upbringing, school, appearance, local culture, religion, beliefs, friends, sports, social expectations, career, levels of success or failure.

> *'I am nobody. Nobody is perfect.*
> *Therefore I am perfect!'*
> Anonymous

EXERCISE
Discover what motivates you

To get to know yourself better, here's a little exercise to discover where you really spend your energy. You may think you know what you value and where you spend your energy, time, and money. Answer these questions honestly and prepare to be surprised. If you have more than one answer for a question, score each answer on a scale 0–10 according to importance, to measure where your energy goes.

◊   What do you love to do in your spare time?

◊   What work would you do even without pay?

◊   What do you spend most of your money on?

◊   What books, magazines, or TV shows interest you?

◊   What do you talk about when you are with friends?

◊   What do you do with most of your energy?

◊   What brings you the greatest sense of fulfillment?

◊   What makes you so happy you lose all track of time?

◊   What makes you feel connected and meaningful?

◊   What or who inspires you more than anyone else?

Your answers should reveal where you invest your energy and what really interests and motivates you. Do your current actions reflect what you truly value? If there's a difference between what you believe you value and how you currently spend your time, energy, and money then perhaps you have some confusion about your identity. Good intentions and high-minded ideals are not enough. How you respond to what happens in life and how you act speaks much louder than words. Even your immune system gets confused.

If you don't know who you truly are, is it possible to genuinely love yourself? When you listen to your thoughts throughout the day, how much time is spent making negative comparisons and self-judgments? Do you focus on how things are less than perfect, rerunning negative movies, listening to derogatory comments and self-flagellation? Unfortunately the 80 trillion cells that make up your body are listening! As they resonate with all the energy and emotions you feel, they receive conflicting messages to move in different directions. Imagine the confusion of those 80 trillion cells. It's amazing they can function at all. A cloud of negative thoughts can obscure the quiet inner source of truth that resides deep within you. Like an internal storm, this cacophony of internal conflicts swirls around the body creating internal noise and disturbance. What if these inner thought clouds could be blown away? What will help reveal the light, the sunshine of your true inner self?

'Only from the heart can you touch the sky.'
Rumi

Your amazing body cells

The incredible organism you call your body depends on all 80 trillion cells working together in cooperative harmony, synchronizing their activities in a miraculous interdependence. Each of your cells could live as a single-cell organism, given the right conditions. Yet evolution led to them choosing to differentiate and work together for more efficient survival advantages. In order to function well this amazingly sophisticated organism requires a coordinated, congruent sense of direction. Your identity, your objectives, and your purpose provide the necessary motivation to move it forward.

What happens if you don't know what you want or where you want to go? What happens when you lose heart, lose the plot, or lose your drive? The 80 trillion cells do a superb job most of the time. However, the white blood cells don't always do their job perfectly. The immune system is affected by many factors: poor diet, vitamin and mineral deficiencies, poisons, heavy metals, genetic disorders, EMF (electromagnetic frequencies), trauma, etc. Have you ever noticed that when you feel stressed or overwhelmed you tend to catch colds more often? People who have a strong motivation to live life fully and be totally authentic, just being who they are, have much stronger immune systems and better health. Simple congruence, being aligned with your core values, seems to work magic. Being able to love yourself in this way may be more important than all the other factors put together.

Stress is now recognized as a key factor in most illnesses, and particularly for the type of tumor I had. Clearly for me, the message was to focus on healing the stressful thoughts and feelings associated with my tumor. Gradually it dawned on me that no matter who or what in the past had influenced me, my current choice of thoughts and feelings belonged to me alone. There was no internal saboteur inside my mind that forced me to continue to think stressful thoughts. I realized my thoughts were my choice. I had the power to govern what I think. The next job was to discover which thoughts needed to change.

*'Courage is resistance to fear,
mastery of fear – not absence of fear.'*
Mark Twain

A long time ago I read an inspiring story in one of Zig Ziglar's books about Major James Nesbeth, who spent seven years as a prisoner of war in North Vietnam. During those seven years he was imprisoned in a cage that was approximately 4½ft (1.25m) high by 5ft (1.5m) long. During the entire time he was imprisoned he saw no one, talked to no one and experienced no physical activity. Many other prisoners held captive in the same conditions lost all hope, went crazy, got sick and died. In order to keep his sanity and his mind active Nesbeth practiced the art of visualization.

Every day in his mind, he imagined every moment of a perfect day of playing golf. He visualized every detail, from getting up in the morning, having breakfast, kissing his wife goodbye and checking the weather to arriving at the golf course and greeting his caddie. Then he would play a full 18-hole game at his favorite green. In his mind he could create the trees, the smell of the freshly trimmed grass, the wind, the songs of the birds. He created different weather conditions – windy spring days, overcast winter days and hot, sunny summer mornings. He felt the grip of the club in his hands as he played his shots in his mind. He would note the set-up, the downswing and the follow-through on each shot. Then he watched the ball arc down the fairway and land at the exact spot he had selected. He did this all in his mind, seven days a week for hours every day, all 18 holes for seven years. When Major Nesbeth was finally released, one of the first things he did when he recovered his strength was to play golf. To his surprise he found that he had cut 20 strokes off his golfing average without having touched a golf club in seven years![1]

Facing any challenge can feel like being trapped or tortured. It can be so easy to become overly focused on your problems and lose perspective. Notice that Major Nesbeth didn't focus on the short-term result of being freed. He took his thoughts to a desirable place of joy and enriched the scene with all the details of life that made it meaningful and compelling. Feeling so positively motivated toward what feels happy, fulfilling and true for you will inspire all the 80 trillion cells of your body to move in the same direction. Although it may not be easy to move your thoughts away from pain, fear, horror, or injustice, what do you have to lose?

> 'All life is an experiment. The more
> experiments you make the better.'
> Ralph Waldo Emerson

A positive future

Do you know what you really want? It is logical to focus on the short-term result: the end of a problem, the healing of an illness or the absence of symptoms. Lots of people say 'I just want to be well.' Notice however that before you faced this particular problem that particular objective probably wasn't on your list. This short-term goal is only a knee-jerk reaction. Although it is a step in the right direction, think more carefully. What do you really want to happen in your life? What would be your equivalent to a movie of playing golf every day? What is truly important and compelling for you? What would make life worth living?

What makes this most effective is to fully flesh out your positive future with details of what it will be like. Your mind doesn't do a good job at telling the difference between reality and imagination – especially if you add lots of details to make it believable. So, imagine the scene as if you are there now: who is with you, what kind of things are you doing, where are you, what feelings do you feel, what is the weather like, and what clothes are you wearing? Can you imagine it happening moment by moment? Don't be content with just thinking you know what you want.

If you take the trouble to imagine what it will really be like, it increases your positive energy, motivation, and healing power. Any resistance to doing this may highlight what could be causing problems. If I had done this at the beginning of my healing journey, I could have saved myself years of searching. Before I was diagnosed, I felt convinced I wanted to get married and have a baby. But I never dwelled on the idea long enough to imagine what that would really be like. I never made compelling happy pictures about how loving my relationship would be or how it would feel to be a mother, or how it would be to care for my baby. I didn't do that, and so I remained unaware of the painful pictures stored in my unconscious mind, radiating negative energy. So as you imagine your positive future scene, do take note of any other thoughts that come into your awareness.

> *'If you are facing in the right direction,
> all you have to do is keep on walking.'*
>
> Zen proverb

EXERCISE
Visualize your future picture

When you have something compelling to look forward to, good long-term reasons to be well, your positive energy creates better cooperation throughout your whole body. If you want all 80 trillion cells to start moving in the same positive direction keep asking yourself: 'What does good look like?' Instead of saying 'I just want to be well' be more specific. For example say, 'I want to feel energized, active, and able to go hiking in the mountains.' Notice how this forms a much more specific picture in your mind. Flesh out your goal by imagining all the things you will be seeing, doing, experiencing, and enjoying once it is achieved. How will you feel? Who will you be with? By the way, what stops you doing some of those activities right now? Here are some questions to help you visualize your future picture:

◊   What do you passionately want to happen in your life?

◊   What is truly important and compelling for you?

◊   Who will be around you and where will you be?

◊   What will experiencing all this make you feel?

◊   Can you imagine all this happening moment by moment?

◊ What does the world around look like, sound like, feel like?

◊ How are you dressed and what clothes are you wearing?

◊ What do you say to yourself and how do you treat yourself now?

◊ What is most important to you now? What are you saying and doing?

◊ How could achieving this move you toward your true purpose?

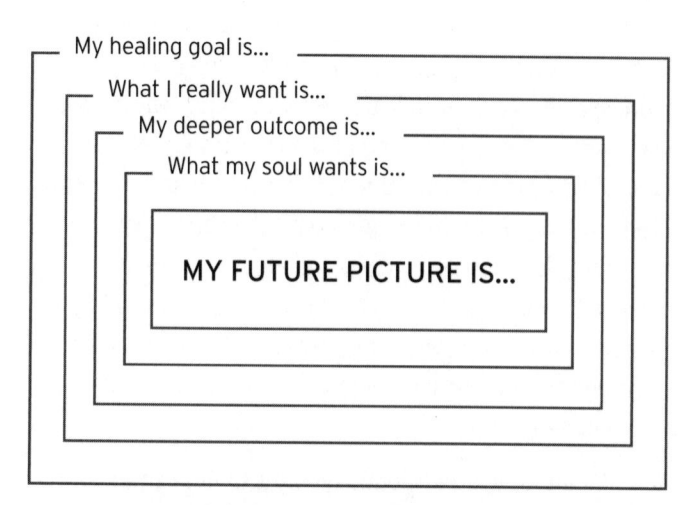

My healing goal is...

What I really want is...

My deeper outcome is...

What my soul wants is...

MY FUTURE PICTURE IS...

Visualizing your perfect future

Take just a few minutes to daydream about your big goal every day and then be sure to let it go. Avoid dwelling on it obsessively or thinking about it all day long. However, writing about it, drawing a picture of it, or creating a visual montage with clippings can help make it more real *and powerful to imagine. The more passion, commitment, and sense of purpose you can add, the more energy flows into healing.*

Reflect for a moment on what would have to change or be different in order to allow this future picture to happen. Begin to notice whatever thoughts come to mind and write those down too. As soon as you start imagining what you do want, you may become more aware of the obstacles that seem to stand in your way.

....

ACID TEST QUESTION
How do you know if you have imagined a future that is right for you?

Thinking about it and daydreaming about it will give you a sense of pleasure and peace, like entering a little oasis of calm amidst chaos. The boost of energy will feel so good; your whole body will enjoy some positive moments and relax.

....

Thinking so positively in the middle of a crisis might seem like an impossible task. But breaking the habits of old thinking just requires a little willingness and some open-minded flexibility. It can be easy to make a new choice. But if you already knew how to do that, if you already had all the answers, you would have already done it. Until now you've been trying to solve the problem with the wrong part of your mind.

Practical Miracles become possible by focusing on the bigger picture and your positive future outcome. Commit to complaining less and appreciating more. Choose to be less in control and more in acceptance. Feel less fear and love more. Keep reading to learn how to turn limited expectations into a vibrant sense of expectancy. When you simply allow yourself to live in the present moment, the future starts looking brighter.

Key points

▶ What you think and feel is totally under your control; you can choose to direct the power of your mind.

▶ Bacteria and viruses cannot thrive unless they have been given the right environment.

▶ The 80 trillion cells that make up your body are listening to everything you think, say, and do.

▶ What feels happy, fulfilling, and true for you will inspire all 80 trillion cells to move in the same direction.

▶ It is a mistake to focus on the short-term result: the end of a problem, the healing of an illness, or the absence of symptoms.

▶ Your mind cannot tell the difference between reality and imagination.

▶ Breaking habits of old thinking requires willingness and open-minded flexibility.

▶ *Practical Miracles* become possible by focusing on the bigger picture and your positive future outcome.

Choice Thoughts

I accept that things have to be this way.

I trust everything will unfold in a better way.

As I become more accepting, I become less controlling.

In order to live in the present, I must let go of the past.

Accepting responsibility means choosing how to respond.

*What has been created can be un-created by
thinking differently.*

*As I complain less and appreciate more,
I fear less and love more.*

Chapter 3

Why Has This Happened and Why Now?

Before you can fix a problem, you must first recognize whatever is broken. Before you can heal your body, you must regard it as sick. Before you can save the world, you must regard it as perishing. Do you notice how this way of thinking reinforces the existence of the negative state? Ironically the more effort you put into fixing something, the more energy you put into the reality of the problem. The more you insist on proving the validity of a problem with tests, evidence, statistics, or measurements, the thicker you build the walls of conviction.

Whether you focus on how to fix it, or on how broken it may be, makes no difference. Both ways of thinking emphasize, confirm and verify the current state of affairs. It's like each thought forms another boulder in your towering mountain of a problem. As you look up at this mountain it takes on more solidity, filling your field of vision, your world, and your identity. As this mountain of a problem seems to define *where* you are, it also starts to define *who* you are. As it obscures your view of the whole picture, it dominates your view of reality. You hesitate to question any thought, or remove any rock, for fear of a tumbling landslide. Your certainty, belief and conviction become as solid as having rocks in your head instead of thoughts.

No perception is indisputable. No measurement is finite. Nothing is set in stone. Everything, even the most verifiable fact, exists in a state of flow. When we view the results of a test done yesterday remember that no one can know for certain whether or not things may have changed for the better or possibly healed. Truth only exists in the moment. What happened yesterday is the past. What's more important than being right about what might have been true in the past, is thinking thoughts of peace in the present. The thoughts we think right now can heal what happens tomorrow and in the future.

> '*Fear less, hope more, whine less, breathe more,*
> *talk less, say more, hate less, love more*
> *and all good things are yours.*'
> Swedish proverb

The body is so amazingly adaptable, it can continue to function for years despite receiving inadequate nutrition, harmful junk food, poisonous substances, EMF (electro-magnetic frequency) pollution, and high levels of stress. The body somehow compensates and continues to do its best just to survive. People who are more resilient and robustly healthy get away with these insults and stresses for longer than those who are more delicate. This makes it less easy to notice the connection between input and result. Plus, for many years the cause of health problems has been wrongly attributed to faulty genes.

Don't genes control everything?

According to molecular biologist Dr. Bruce Lipton, genes are merely the reproductive organs of the cell. A cell can live for two months after DNA is removed. Rather than DNA predetermining destiny or causing disease, the genes merely carry 'information.' Genes primarily hold the information blueprint for making different types of protein molecules: the building blocks of cells. But genes do nothing until they are switched on. We can have the gene associated with a particular disease and never turn it on. In fact 95 percent of all cancer has no hereditary connection. When children are adopted into families that have cancer, the percentage of those children who get cancer is the same as any child born naturally into that family, even though those children's genetic inheritance did not include cancer genes. Therefore the factors that influence a gene to switch on must be learned via family dynamics, perceptions, beliefs, and attitudes in the environment.[1]

The solution is not as simple as finding the one gene that causes cancer and switching it off. Breast cancer, for example, involves over 189 genetic errors. According to Lipton, whether a gene gets switched on or off depends on the 'regulatory sequences' or the spaces in between the genes. These sequences must be precise or the end result is completely different. As scientific researcher Peter Fraser says in *The Living Matrix*, each gene represents only one book in the vast library of DNA. But the genes contained in the human DNA library are the same genes used by all other animals, all the way down to earthworms. How does the body know which books to take out of that library? What process governs the sequence that switches a gene on or off?[2, 3]

> *'It is not the strongest of the species that survive, nor the most intelligent, but the one most responsive to change.'*
> Charles Darwin

When biochemist John Cairns experimented on a colony of Escherichia coli (E.coli), his results were surprising. These particular E.coli bacteria have no genes for creating lactase, the enzyme that breaks down milk sugar. Cairns immersed this colony of E.coli in milk, where they had nothing else to eat. Immediately the genes began to mutate in order to create lactase, so that the E.coli could digest the milk sugar! Even though they did not have the necessary genes, these cells quickly learned what to do in order to survive. They wrote a new book in response to the food crisis in their environment. If a simple bacteria can do this, then it follows that more sophisticated human body cells can do this too. [4]

Lipton has long maintained that genes change according to environmental influence. He says what governs the regulatory sequence is the membrane between the cell and the outside fluids. Receptors in the membrane of the cell not only control the cell but also alter how the whole genome gets expressed. So he concludes that the environment outside the cell determines the content of the fluids inside the cell and whether or not the genes get switched on or off.

Why is the effect of the environment important to know?

What is true for cells may also hold true for groups of people. Have you ever noticed that people respond to stimuli in their surrounding environment and culture? Sitting in a stadium of excited sports enthusiasts cheering the teams to win is highly contagious. Political rallies whip up emotions, influence beliefs, and sway decisions of the crowd. Even visiting a site where powerful events occurred long ago holds a lingering energy that resonates long after the events.

When a pregnant mother experiences fear, the environment of her whole womb is flooded with adrenalin and so the baby's body is filled with adrenalin too. Consequently the baby's hindbrain (governing balance and coordination for fight and flight) develops and grows faster and bigger than the forebrain (which governs cognitive, sensory and motor function). So what happens in the mother's environment directly affects the baby's development, predisposition, and nature. According to Lipton, the baby in the womb tries to prepare itself for the world to be faced after birth. The environment of this baby will make him or her a born fighter. So pregnant mothers who live in fear produce warrior babies[1].

When fear, anger or rage floods the system, the negative energy stimulates the hindbrain and shuts down the forebrain. In the middle of rage, the anger seems to cause a temporary frontal lobotomy. Anger and fear make it difficult to think straight, be flexible, see another's point of view or apply the mind to discovering what needs to be healed. However, many people have such a well-developed habit of suppressing their feelings that they are not aware of this anger. Outwardly they seem cool and dissociated. Inwardly the anger gets pushed into the body. Then it gets expressed in passive-aggressive ways toward others and toward their bodies. Whether anger is expressed or suppressed, the body suffers.

> *'Every minute you are angry, you lose sixty seconds of happiness.'*
> Ralph Waldo Emerson

On a more positive note, the environment around spiritual masters can uplift the mood of all the people in a room by their mere presence, their smile or the energy that comes through their eyes. Perhaps you have sensed the tranquility and calmness in cathedrals or mosques where years of prayers have left a resonance of love and reverence. When you align positive thoughts with your inner purpose you create a protective environment that encourages healing throughout your body.

Choosing better thoughts

The positive resonance left behind in particular environments may be due to the number of people who coordinated their thoughts on a repeated basis. The more people who collectively choose better thoughts, the more impact this has on positive change. History is full of events and wars where the influence of combined thought fields drove people's energy in disruptive directions. Maybe now is the time for humanity to make the choice to collectively focus thoughts in a positive direction. Why not start at home and practice directing your thoughts to be more positively productive?

'*Seek not to change the world, but choose
to change your mind about the world.*'
A Course in Miracles, Anon

Scientific research says that every cell in your body could live alone as a single cell organism with an infinite lifespan, if it has all the nutrients and conditions it needs. As Dr. Deepak Chopra says in his book *Quantum Healing*, 'each cell in the body renews itself in a never-ending stream of change.' A new layer of skin grows every day, new stomach lining every five days, new soft tissue every three months, and new bone cells every six months. So the body you had yesterday is not the same body you have today. Considering how the body originates from just two tiny cells – one egg and one sperm – the complexity of how they multiply and differentiate into 80 trillion cells working together so harmoniously is a miracle.[5]

If almost every cell in our bodies is replaced every six months then the bodies we have now are not the same bodies we had last year. This must also mean that miraculous healing power is available every day. Whenever a cell replaces itself, it follows the blueprint to grow a brand new cell. Therefore whenever a symptom is created, the body should know how to un-create it. Doesn't that mean the body should look brand new and fresh as a baby every six months, instead of aging? Scars and wrinkles should disappear instead of becoming permanent fixtures? Curiously, research shows that people with multiple personalities or 'dissociated identity disorder' have different symptoms when they switch between one identity and another. In the space of a few minutes, as the switch occurs, the person may suddenly need glasses, go blind, deaf, demonstrate allergies to different things, suffer anesthesia, paralysis, different measurements of blood pressure, blood sugar levels (diabetes) as well as scars that disappear and reappear with the alternating personalities. Doesn't that suggest some kind of direct link between consciousness and the body?[6]

Most of the time our immune system does a brilliant job of protecting the body from disease and destroying aberrant cells and foreign invaders on a daily basis, as long as it can follow the blueprint and correctly identify what belongs and what does not belong inside. So that begs the question: why don't tumors return to normal healthy cell growth? What stops the immune system from preventing tumor cells creating more tumor cells? Perhaps the secret behind spontaneous remissions will soon be discovered.

Not knowing *how* to do it

Having a clear idea of what you want doesn't mean you necessarily know how to do it. Lots of people get stuck when they focus on needing to know exactly what to do at each step. The desire for predictability and security leads to trying to rationally plan everything in advance in order to achieve a guaranteed result. People long for certainty so that they can follow logical steps and make the 'right decisions.' But life flows in unpredictable ways and follows a zigzag path. It helps to remember you can make lots of mistakes and still achieve your outcome.

'Life is pretty simple: you do some stuff. Most fails. Some works. You do more of what works. If it works big, others quickly copy it. Then you do something else. The trick is the doing something else.'
Leonardo da Vinci

It has been estimated that people think between 12,000 and 65,000 thoughts per day and the increase in information to be processed means the number is going up. The average person thinks about 12,000 thoughts per day, while deeper thinkers may think more than 60,000. That roughly works out to about one thought per second or 1,000 thoughts per hour. If you meditate you might be well aware of this thought traffic constantly flowing through your mind.

The first few times a thought travels in a particular direction, it leaves only a few footprints behind. With each repetition, those thoughts begin to create a habitual pathway. As you add more evidence, rational deductions, logic and reasons, the path becomes a paved road. Gradually, with more use, more emotion and more conviction, those well-traveled roads expand into four-lane highways in your mind. The thoughts flow so fast down these highways, there is no time to pause and reconsider. Consequently 95 percent of those 60,000 thoughts merely follow the same route as the day before. The neural pathways that get used most often flow the fastest. The constant repetition lulls the brain into believing that these thoughts equal reality, a comfort zone of certainty.

Thought waves radiate energy

Each thought produces waves of energy that radiate out into space. This energy converts into mass: ($E=MC^2$). As each thought wave radiates out, it resonates with whatever matches that thought, selecting from millions of other possibilities in the environment. The information that matches your thought reflects a vibration back to your senses. Then your eyes, ears and other senses recognize and verify your version of what you think is out there. Your thoughts govern your perception. This explains why people tend to see only what they want to see.

Scientists used to think that sight depended on light being passed through the lens of the eye to receptors on the retina. The image was then projected upside down somewhere near the back of the brain, due to the refraction of the lens. The famous neurosurgeon Karl Pribram theorizes something much more interesting. He says the brain and the receptors of your retina are like sensitive tuning instruments that respond to wave interference. Wave interference is like the way strings in a piano resonate to certain sound frequencies. Instead of seeing images in the back of the brain, the receptors resonate with certain interference patterns. Then the brain creates a virtual image of what you are looking at. The brain projects this virtual image out in space in the same place as the original object. So you think you see it. Similar to a hologram, the lens of your eye picks up selected interference patterns and converts them into three-dimensional images to make it even more believable.[7]

This explains why babies have to learn how to see, even though the lens in each of their eyes has perfect focus. When newborn babies first open their eyes, the genes in the visual cortex start forming connections. When the baby gazes at an object, millions of signals start entering the retina. The more frequently a particular signal comes in, the more that connection is strengthened. If the baby does not get the right kind of visual input during the first critical months of life, the baby will never learn to see properly.[8]

Another example is the curious story reported by Charles Darwin. When his big clipper ship the *Beagle* arrived in

Patagonia, he rowed ashore with his men in small boats. Some of the islanders rowed out to meet them in their canoes and asked, 'How did you get here? We know these islands and we've never seen you before.' Darwin pointed to the *Beagle*, but they couldn't see the ship. They had no concept in their mind that such a thing could exist. Until Darwin rowed them out to the ship and took them aboard the deck, explaining it was just a 'large canoe,' their brains and eyes just deleted the information that didn't fit their reality.[9]

Perhaps this might also explain how someone can paint the whole world black and only see negative things when they are in a bad mood. They are choosing to resonate only with what matches their mood. Conversely, it also means you could choose to see everything as beautiful.

> 'The sun shines and warms and lights us and we have no curiosity to know why this is so; but we ask the reason of all evil, of pain, and hunger, and mosquitoes and silly people.'
>
> Ralph Waldo Emerson

How the brain is programmed

Your brain has been wired to detect any possible threat to your survival. Unfortunately that means 70-90 percent of those thoughts focus on negative possibilities.[10] You wouldn't be able to cross the street if this were not so. Every second, millions of bits of information bombard your senses: sight, sound, taste, touch, and smell. Because your conscious mind can't process the massive amount of incoming information, it must delete everything that it deems less important. If it didn't, the brain would be so overwhelmed that it couldn't function. The conscious mind can only focus on fewer than 10 items per second. In order to survive, your mind filters, focuses and chooses what seems to be most important, according to how it has been preprogrammed. Of course, each person chooses different items. So who has the correct version of reality?

Perhaps an even more important question is, who programmed your mind? You did. From the first moment you opened your eyes as a baby, you made decisions about whether you liked what you saw. You judged whether things were friendly or threatening, safe or dangerous, attractive or repulsive, good or bad, right or wrong, etc.

Until the age of six, a child's brain operates in a trance state of *delta* and *theta* brain waves, sleeping, dreaming and imagining. Children soak everything up like sponges, absorbing as much wisdom as possible through a process called introjection. By watching the behavior of their caretakers, they swallow and absorb their values and standards, unconsciously. These ideas get incorporated into the young brain without any rational process of evaluation. The child has no sense of boundaries and little defense. The only way to have any control over the environment is to absorb everything. This explains how the parents' attitudes, beliefs and values seed the cloud of neurons that begin to structure in the child's brain. It also explains why the journey of discovery may need to revisit these important origins.

Garbage in, garbage out

Your mind is like a computer being filled with data every day of your life. Few stop to question the validity of the original input data. Few dare to challenge the reasons and deductions that have long been accepted as fact. Few comprehend that the images being observed have actually been created in the mind first. Few realize that the conscious mind is a waking trance state. It's only when you wake up and ask the questions: 'Who am I? Why am I here? What is my purpose?' that positive change becomes possible.

As the brain evolves over time, the intricate structure of neurons grows and develops according to new input and usage. At first, thoughts form slowly, joining one word to another as language is mastered, until whole sentences start to carve out grooves in the mind. The more the words and thoughts get repeated, the deeper the groove. Each repetition makes the thought more believable and more real until the conditioned grooves become like railroad tracks, taking the train of thoughts to the same destination each time. People who are multilingual notice that using different languages changes the way they express themselves, how they feel and even how they experience reality.[11]

In *The Brain that Changes Itself*, psychiatrist Norman Doidge says people often relive memories from the past instead of just remembering them.[12] The more you repeat a thought or memory with intense emotion, the more real it seems. In fact, the brain does a very poor job of differentiating between what's real and what's imagined. Brainwashing works by reinforcing particular thoughts repeatedly over time, usually under stress. The brain cannot function efficiently when it's confused and so it quickly grabs on to whatever promises certainty and relief. The brain hates confusion so much it tries to avoid it by accepting the brainwashing as true. However brainwashing doesn't have to be negative. A similar process can be used for a positive effect. Adequate reinforcing and repetition of a positive change in thinking not only redefines the original event, but also changes the brain structure, increasing conviction about the positive belief. So people seeking healing could benefit from repetitively choosing positive thoughts with passion, reality, congruence, and conviction.

Evolution of thinking

According to research undertaken by IONS (Institute of Noetic Science), the input to the brain during the early formative years builds a structure of 'information' that explains reality according to whatever is experienced. Education adds to that structure until the brain becomes more or less satisfied about what is what. If new information challenges the existing programming then the brain will resist taking it in. No matter how much truth, evidence or proof there may be, the brain persists in holding on to the original programming.[13] Once the brain has decided which version of reality to believe, the doors close. You may have met people like this. David Dunning, professor of social psychology at Cornell, says:

Even if you are just the most honest, impartial person that you could be, you would still have a problem: namely, when your knowledge or expertise is imperfect, you really don't know it. Left to your own devices, you just don't know it. We're not very good at knowing what we don't know.[14]

Your comfort zone

Over time our brains build comfort zones according to our selected versions of reality. Each experience and each decision defines our perception of life. This thinking structure gives us the sense of stability necessary to feel secure and safe. Even if our version of reality is less than pleasant, at least it's the reality we know. No matter how uncomfortable we feel, the brain resists any attempt to change these perceptions once the structure of our 'comfort zones' has been formed. In every moment, we have the opportunity to choose new thought energy waves moving in either a positive or negative direction. However, the survival instinct of the brain chooses to sort for possible danger first. So unless we retrain our brains, the habitual and negative thoughts predominate. Could this explain the common tendency to judge, complain, be skeptical, look at the downside, and be pessimistic?

What if each person has been allotted only a certain amount of thought energy during a particular lifetime? Once you have used up all that thought energy, the story is over. Suppose those thoughts have been invested in two different bank accounts: positive thoughts and negative thoughts. Which one would gather more interest? If you invest your thoughts positively you get great returns. Accrue negative thoughts and accumulate trouble. It just makes more sense to invest your thought energy more wisely. The quality of your thoughts produces your abundance in life.

Most people just allow their brains to run wild, like a computer with no one at the controls. Few pay attention to unspoken thoughts, even fewer have learned how to resolve what causes negative thinking. Most people make the mistake of believing their thoughts are based on objective reality. With little awareness of the thoughts passing through the mind, everything seems okay until something goes wrong. Until you have examined, resolved, and revised your habitual version of reality, the old familiar grooves of thinking continue, producing the same feelings and results whether you are conscious of these or not. In later chapters you will find some insights and strategies for managing your thoughts. It is possible to update your old thought programs with improved ideas and concepts that better match your inner truth and wisdom.

The stable 'comfort zone' in the brain has inherent flaws because it was built on limited information, full of misperceptions. How could the young child who programmed your brain correctly interpret and understand what was really going on? What kind of influence came from the caretakers in the environment? The brain continues to delete, distort, and generalize all new input according to the original acquired beliefs and values from early childhood. Your sense of reality is built on this early template. Over time the repetition of those errors and mistakes has created uncomfortable comfort zones: the source of stressful negative energy.

Thoughts shape your perception

The thoughts you think determine how you perceive the world, how you respond to what's going on, what you choose to do, and how you shape your life experience. Did you ever play 'spot the red convertible' during long car journeys as a child? Before the game started, you didn't notice them at all, but once you chose to look for red convertibles, you saw them everywhere! It works the same way with all your thoughts. What you choose to put your focus on makes you more aware of what resonates with those thoughts in your environment. Shift your thinking and what you notice around you will change. Your perceptions will not only register different aspects of the environment but also make new meanings of everything you see.

This power of thought works better than a magic pill and it has no side effects. Like the famous scene in the iconic movie *The Matrix* it boils down to a simple choice between two alternatives: do you want to take the blue pill or the red pill? The blue pill allows you to continue to invest in present illusions of reality and remain entranced by a virtual world. Taking the red pill means you choose to awaken, see, hear, feel, and know the truth of reality.

Every problem presents a similar choice. Either invest your thoughts like a victim: moaning, complaining, blaming, and feeling powerless; or choose to think like a hero who takes responsibility, faces the demons, finds a way through, and overcomes the obstacles to reach success. No one can tell you what to think or how to feel. Bad things do happen. Bad things happen to good people. Chaos, disaster, misfortune, loss, injustice, illness, earthquakes, tsunamis, terrorism, and war do happen on this planet. What is the best way to meet such challenges in life? What needs to change? What would have to be different for you?

....

ACID TEST QUESTION
Where have you been investing your thoughts?

Just listen to yourself or ask your close friends and family. How many of your comments sound like moaning, complaining, whining, or blaming? How many sound full of courage, trust, good humor, empowerment, and authenticity? Do you feel more like a victim or the hero?

....

Life will never be the same again

Many people overlook the fact that every problem also represents a departure; a threshold has been crossed. Not only have you fallen out of your comfort zone, there's no way back. Life will never be the same again. At first, this might feel like loss. You may need to go through a necessary grieving process. Some cherished dream may have been shattered. Your feelings need to be listened to, acknowledged, and felt. Fear, anger, sadness, guilt, and regret all have an appropriate time and place. But that isn't the end of the story. After you feel your feelings appropriately, move on to make better choices.

Have you ever noticed how dealing with a crisis makes life less boring? People hate being bored. With amusing irony, the Chinese like to say, 'May you have an interesting life.' Certainly having to deal with crisis makes life more interesting: full of change and growth opportunities. It might look like there's no solution: nothing will ever change and nothing can be done. The opponents seem too strong and too difficult to defeat. Yet the true hero never gives up, but musters some kind of persistent doggedness and keeps plugging away even when all seems hopeless.

The hero's journey requires having the courage to step into the unknown. The way forward may not be clear, but conventional thinking hasn't worked. So doing what has always been done no longer makes sense. Despite not having clear steps to follow, you need to move in the direction of your positive future. Using your desired destination to guide you forward, just keep adjusting your path until you make progress in the right direction.

People who survive major challenges: illness, war, accident, loss, or repeated failure, make those events the major turning points of their lives. They redefine who they are and what they do and why they do it, in the most positive and humble way. Such people persevere, trusting and having faith that whatever their journey entails, they will prevail in the end and reach the desired destination, even if it looks a bit different from what they originally envisioned. They let go of their plan and trust, taking each moment one at a time. They have gratitude for the wonder of the experience itself. The journey itself is the purpose.

Resilience thrives on being able to say 'yes' to life with love, openness, happiness, and the spirit of giving. Just allow the journey to continue to unfold, and access the deep inner courage and wisdom you have within you. There's no longer any urgency because there's nowhere to go. The journey home itself is the gift and destination. All paths lead home. Every miracle begins with a change of thought. The shift in consciousness required is the return to wholeness.

Key points

▶ Genes change, switching on or off, according to environmental influence and they can learn what to do in order to survive.

▶ Anger and fear shut down the brain, make it difficult to think, be flexible or see any other point of view.

▶ You think between 12,000 and 65,000 thoughts per day, one thought per second, which is at least 1,000 thoughts per hour.

▶ The brain avoids being overwhelmed by incoming information by deleting most of it according to pre-programming.

....

- Like a computer being filled with data, the mind accepts information as fact without question or challenge.

- The brain does a poor job of differentiating between what is real or imagined.

- Until the old ideas have been changed or resolved, the highways of habitual thinking predominate and continue.

- People who survive major challenges make those events into major turning points in their life.

....

Choice Thoughts

No perception is indisputable.

Miraculous healing power is available every day.

I can make lots of mistakes and still achieve my goal.

The thoughts I think determine how I perceive the world.

I feel my feelings and move on to make better choices.

This could be a major turning point in my life.

I let go of my plan and trust moment by moment.

Chapter 4

Mindfulness: The Key Resource of Resilience

Many people live life like hamsters, jumping on the same wheel of thoughts day after day, endlessly chasing what seems to promise happiness. People spend 70 percent of their lives watching reruns of the same thoughts again and again. Like an internal hard drive, our minds record, store, and project the movies of our choice: misery to happiness. These dramas, love stories, adventures, comedies, crimes of passion, triumphs over the odds, healing crises, or tragedies seem very real. The funny thing is that most people forget they hold the remote control. When you face a crisis, remember the power to change the channel is in your hands.

Even a small change in thinking has profound effects, but the bigger the shift in thinking, the more dramatic the transformation. The problem is that most of the mind stays preoccupied rerunning old movies, full of old, unconscious thinking programmed in the distant past. If you always think the way you've always thought before, how can anything ever change? Watching these old reruns again and again, the story always has the same ending. To stop repeating the same old problem, there must be a shift in thinking.

Thoughts create emotions

Unaware of how the unconscious mind works, people go looking for the troublesome thoughts in their conscious mind. This is a mistake! No one gets up in the morning and consciously decides to be ill. The famous psychiatrist, who specialized in medical hypnosis, Dr. Milton Erickson said people have problems due to being out of rapport with their unconscious minds.[1] The aberrant thought process begins in childhood with some slightly negative idea, a mistake, limiting belief or traumatic event. These continue to fester in the unconscious mind, selectively gathering more evidence from life experiences to support what was not true in the first place. Surprisingly, the happiest childhoods can breed such thoughts, just as well as traumatic childhoods.

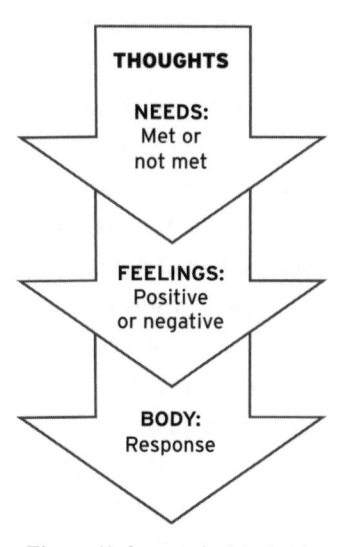

The path from mind to body

As is shown in the preceding diagram, with every thought, there is an associated feeling. When our needs are being met, positive thoughts and positive feelings of satisfaction, peace, and happiness follow. Everything is okay. When our needs do not get met, the thoughts turn judgmental, defensive, and protective. Negative feelings result: fear, anger, loss, sadness, etc. Emotions trigger chemical reactions by releasing hormones throughout the body. Positive emotions such as compassion enhance life and health. Negative emotions such as anger create immediate tension and stress, weakening the immune system and lowering resistance. Because the thoughts we think create our emotions, learning to be mindful is crucial to wellbeing.

'Pain exists only in resistance.
Joy exists only in acceptance.
Painful situations that you heartily
accept become joyful.
Joyful situations that you do not
accept become painful.
There is no such thing as a bad experience.
Bad experiences are simply the creations of your
resistance to what is.'
Rumi

Raising awareness

Resilience requires becoming more aware of the thoughts that pass through your mind. Mindfulness means learning to pay attention to your thoughts, emotions and words in each moment. Most conscious everyday thoughts cause no problems. It's the unconscious thoughts that need careful attention. Because the conscious and unconscious mind use the same brain cells, discovering unconscious thoughts is as easy as asking a question. For example, just think of your phone number and say it out loud. A split second ago, that number was in your unconscious. Do you notice what direction it came from? Notice that as soon as you stop focusing on your phone number it disappears back into the unconscious. Did it go back to the same place?

A curious fact about the brain is that it can't resist answering a question. Like a computer, as soon as a question is asked, it goes on a search for an answer. The conscious mind loves to come up with quick answers. The predictability of an answer, something that sounds like typical everyday thinking, habitual reasoning, or negative judgment reveals that the conscious mind replied. However, by asking the right type of questions, you can access the unconscious and higher conscious thoughts. One of the best times to do this is late at night before you go to sleep. Tune in to your heart and connect with feelings of love and peace. Pose a compassionate question about what insights you really need to know. Your mind may supply the answer in your dreams, or you may wake up just knowing the answer. The conscious mind is most quiet in the early hours of the morning so this is the best time to listen; then you will receive new insights, recall distant memories, or make helpful connections.

EXERCISE
First aid for stress

Whenever you have to face a challenging, stressful situation practice this simple way to calm your mind. Focus on breathing deep into your belly. Place one hand on your upper chest, the other on your belly. Make sure you are expanding your belly as far as you can with long, slow, deep breaths. This expands the diaphragm and sends messages to the brain to calm down. At the same time lift your chin and raise your eyes above the horizon. Avoid letting your chin and eyes sink down. Force your mind to focus on something positive, either in the immediate environment or a completely imaginary scene. Then keep repeating your favorite positive mantra to yourself. Choose something that immediately uplifts you, for example:

◊　　*I can do this.*

◊　　*All is okay.*

◊　　*Calm and relaxed.*

◊　　*Love God.*

◊　　*Miracles happen.*

◊　　*This too shall pass.*

◊　　*I am safe.*

'No one saves us but ourselves. No one can and no one may. We ourselves must walk the path.'
Buddha

During my healing journey, I wasn't aware of how much energy I was investing in trying to heal my tumor. Wanting to heal sounded like such a good outcome. For several years, I didn't notice that my desire to get rid of my tumor was also a self-attack in disguise. Then early one morning, I heard a very enraged internal voice inside my head silently screaming, 'I just want to be rid of this nightmare!' Sensing the energy of extreme frustration behind this thought, I recognized an obvious source of inner stress. Thoughts like this must be raising the production of my stress hormones. But what could I do? The voice was telling the truth! I did want to get rid of my tumor. There was no point lying to myself. My unconscious knew how I felt. Intellectually I could understand that healing would require finding a peaceful alternative: accepting the tumor. But how could I get to a place of accepting the unacceptable? How could I stop *wanting* to get rid of the problem?

I chose to look back over all the years I had spent experimenting with different healing approaches. As I reviewed all the things I had learned, I began to appreciate how much I had grown and developed. Slowly it dawned on me how many good things had come about. With deep gratitude, I thought of all the great teachers and wonderful people I had met who had helped me in so many ways. I was touched to know that people in a special prayer group included me in their healing prayers. I would never have attended so many workshops, traveled to faraway places, and experienced all the adventures of learning that led to a whole new career, without the tumor's motivation. In fact, the tumor had been my guide, my best friend all along. It forced me to grow and develop in ways I would never have imagined. What touched me deeply was the realization that owing to all this I had reached a place of actually liking myself. To my wonderment, I felt happy being me.

Luckily I'd also learned how to manage my symptoms so well that the tumor no longer intruded on my life. But I wondered why it was still present. Could there possibly be more to learn, more places to explore? Was it trying to keep me humble? It had done such a good job so far that I decided that I could trust it without knowing the answer. So all my newfound gratitude and appreciation helped me reach a place where I could genuinely say to myself, 'I give my tumor permission to stay to the end of my days.' From that day, I accepted the tumor as my friend. Then a curious thing happened: I forgot about it! I got on with my life as normal. Six months later, my routine test results showed no evidence of the tumor anymore. The blood test measurements were totally normal. But the most extraordinary thing was that it no longer mattered to me whether it had healed or not!

> *'Every situation, properly perceived,*
> *becomes an opportunity to heal.'*
> A Course in Miracles, Anon

Interpreting symptoms

One blessing of illness is that symptoms provide immediate clues about the thoughts lurking in the unconscious mind. Each symptom reveals the presence of specific negative thoughts asking to be noticed. The first clue lies in the location of the problem: the body part affected is a metaphor. What role does that part (organ, tissue, gland, or fluid) perform in normal life from inception onward? What no longer functions the way it should? Sometimes a major illness causes normal life to grind to a halt.[2]

Here's a very brief example of interpreting such body symptoms. After enduring an extremely difficult divorce, a woman became ill and received a diagnosis of bowel cancer. Her whole divorce experience felt quite indigestible because she could not let go of her regret, her loss, or her rage. On a physical level, the large intestine's job is to reclaim the water from the waste products of digestion before getting rid of the compacted debris. Problems usually cause blockage: constipation or diarrhea. In this case there was also an overgrowth of aberrant cells.

On a metaphoric level, the large intestine could have been holding on to negative ideas and bad thoughts instead of letting go. Holding on to the negative is the opposite of goodness and innocence and therefore leads to feeling guilty. Guilt also indicates low self-worth. The excessive growth suggested the presence of negative thoughts that had become obsessive. She admitted what she could not reclaim were her feelings of innocence. Her self-worth had been shattered. Her guilt and repetitive negative thoughts were multiplying faster than the cancer cells and obstructing her ability to let go.

By interpreting the symptoms she began to recognize the connection between her thoughts and her illness. This helped her feel more in control of what had happened and empowered her to take more responsibility. She was able to clarify more precisely what inner changes she needed to make in order to heal. This gave her a practical focus: how to restore her sense of self-esteem.

If you have bodily symptoms, think about which part of the body is affected. Focus on that part of the body and brainstorm all the functions and metaphorical meanings this part might have for you. Look up the function in an encyclopedia, on Wikipedia, or refer to one of the recommended books about interpreting body symptoms. While knowledge of anatomy helps, most people know that the stomach digests food, lungs take in air, feet move you forward, etc. Take a moment to write down all the personal associations you have for that body part. For example, you might have feet just like your mother's, so a problem with your feet might mean you have absorbed her beliefs about taking steps forward in life. Any clue provides a good starting point. You might also find helpful some of the recommended books listed under 'Interpreting symptoms' (see page 269).

> 'As is the human body, so is the cosmic body.
> As is the human mind, so is the cosmic mind.
> As is the microcosm, so is the macrocosm.'
> Ayurvedic saying

Metaphorical meanings

Think laterally: what issues might relate to the action of this body part? For example, problems in the stomach might relate to being unable to digest what is happening in your life. An inflamed stomach ulcer might indicate feeling inflamed with anger about some indigestible event. Taking in air is obviously a matter of life or death. Could a lung problem be saying you feel choked up about something of vital importance? If you can't breathe properly, could it be about not fully participating in life?

Interpreting symptoms varies from person to person because the metaphors people associate with body parts are unique to each person. Serious illnesses often involve multiple symptoms and communications, like a backlog of issues that were never properly resolved. The complex symptoms involved with illness are like a nest full of hungry baby birds, each screaming for attention and nourishment. To feed each of those baby birds you need to deal with the issues they are screaming about. When the communication receives an appropriate response, when the issues are resolved, the underlying stress lifts off. When the body's immune system is unencumbered it can get on with the job of correction.

Deeper meanings behind your problem may be revealed by what you have been stopped from doing. This could be one particular activity, or many activities. Serious illnesses and accidents usually put a 'stop' to normal life. Whatever you can no longer do could reveal an important part of the issue. When you love doing a particular sport or some other activity and can no longer do it, this might not make sense at first. But could there be a hidden reason why you wanted to pull back, have a rest, give that up or deny yourself pleasure? Perhaps it has to do with other people who are involved. Pose your mind a question about what could possibly be the reason. Make a list of all the ridiculous and possible reasons as well as any inner conflicts you might feel about the activity.

ACID TEST QUESTION
How do you know if you've arrived at the correct metaphorical meaning?

The truth is you can never be sure. It is not an exact science. Different people will come up with different meanings. There could be several layers to the problem and several metaphors could apply. If a metaphor provides clues to the original cause or points you in the right direction to look for beliefs, decisions, or emotions then it is useful. Often the metaphor only becomes clear with hindsight.

An accident with a message

Most people think accidents are exempt from any kind of personal responsibility. Yet it's possible to make associations and reclaim your power if you begin to understand how an accident might be mirroring your thinking. One day, my curiosity was sparked by an odd remark made by a client with a stubborn chronic back problem. He grumbled, 'My back has never been right since that accident 30 years ago!' He had previously maintained that the cause of his back trouble related to a recent hang-gliding mishap so this remark surprised me. Further questioning revealed an extraordinary story.

One morning he had set out to make a long car journey. While driving down a six-lane road leading out of London, the heavy traffic had slowed to a crawl. For some reason, on the other side of the street, a woman decided to walk across this six-lane road, in between the cars and hidden from his view. Because he didn't see her coming, when she suddenly stepped in front of him, his car hit her and knocked off her feet. An ambulance was called and she was taken to hospital. Although she wasn't badly hurt, he felt so shocked by the incident he had to go home to recover.

Later the same day, he decided to set off again to make the previously aborted journey. This time he got onto the main highway and was progressing at top speed. On the opposite side of the motorway, another driver suddenly realized she was driving in the wrong direction. Unfortunately, she made the curious decision to drive across the grass median and cross the path of all the oncoming cars in order to correct her mistake! The inevitable crash was truly devastating. He got pushed through his windshield with serious injuries. 'It was just bad luck!' he said. But could the coincidence of two separate accidents, both involving women crossing his path, have another meaning?

After just a few questions, he confessed the Mercedes sports car he had been driving that day was borrowed from his mother. At that time, he and his mother were clashing violently over what direction he should take in life. She totally opposed his desires and decisions. Being quite ambitious, he felt her stupid rules were blocking his way forward. So as he collided against her wishes while judging her as useless, crazy and stupid, he also collided physically using her car. Suddenly, so many years later, he finally understood the connection and felt very amused.

'Anyone can become angry – that is easy.
But to be angry with the right person, to the
right degree, at the right time, for the right
purpose, and in the right way – this is not easy.'
Aristotle

Right-sided and left-sided symptoms

In psychology the theory of left-brain and right-brain dominance is based on the lateralization of brain function. Neuropsychologist and Nobel laureate Roger W. Sperry discovered the two halves of the cortex specialized in different functions. When he cut the corpus callosum that joins the two, his patients had difficulty accessing specific information. Out of this work it has been surmised that people have a preference or dominance of left or right. The left-brain is adept at logic, vocabulary, analytical thinking, mathematics, and linear reasoning, while the right brain is best at expressive and creative tasks, reading emotions, recognizing faces, music, art, intuition, and lateral thinking. Underneath the brain, the nerves coming from the left and right hemispheres cross over to serve the opposite side of the body. So the left brain serves the right side of the body and the right brain serves the left.

Metaphorically, this is why the left and right sides of your body get associated with different meanings. Right-sided problems often have more to do with the masculine: work and career, while left-sided problems have to do with the feminine: creativity and relationships. When your feet or legs do not want to move forward, notice which foot is affected. The side of the body gives a clue about the steps you do not want to take, or the steps you wish you had not taken.

Example: a left-sided problem

A woman with a recurring infection in her left ear had difficulty identifying what the symptom might mean. The ear infection was inflamed, hot and angry, and obviously indicated a metaphor to do with listening. The left ear connects more directly with the side of the brain governing the intuition, emotions, creativity, music, art, lateral thinking, relationships, and the feminine. But none of these connected with any associated meanings for her. Was there something she wanted to hear? Something she didn't like hearing? Further exploration revealed her problem was about listening to the constant negative chattering of her mind. This immediately made sense to her. She admitted to being an expert at judgment, self-blame and self-flagellation. Her internal dialogue spoke more harshly to her than anyone in her life. She hated listening to the constant barrage of destructive angry criticism.

Once she acknowledged the source of her ear problem, she chose to moderate her internal dialogue. She made friends with this alienated part of her unconscious mind. She did her best to understand its reasons and positive intentions. Instead of yelling and using bad language, she invited it to speak with a softer voice. The same messages could be delivered, but with kind words. Once her inner voice felt she was listening, it became less judging and more encouraging. Gradually she felt more at peace and the ear symptoms settled down.

> 'He who smiles rather than rages
> is always the stronger.'
> Japanese proverb

Example: a right-sided problem

After undergoing urgent surgery and radiotherapy for lymphoma, a highly successful barrister felt mystified about what had caused this life-threatening illness. He loved his work, loved his family and lived a good life. His story began after he received a small scratch on his right shin while playing sports. It refused to heal and instead swelled into an ugly infection, requiring excision, stitches, and antibiotic injections. A few months later, an ominous rubbery lump appeared on his right thigh, which was diagnosed as lymphoma. He immediately went for the recommended treatment: surgery and radiotherapy. But although his treatment was deemed successful, he worried that the lymphoma might come back. He needed to know why this had occurred. What were the underlying mental or emotional causes of his lymphoma?

The symptoms on the right leg indicated something to do with taking steps forward in his career and work. As lymphoma is a highly aggressive form of cancer, the issues involved must be highly important: a life-or-death matter. The inflammation suggested anger, the cancer suggested loops of obsessive thoughts had been multiplying. The danger could spread throughout his whole system, but so far, it focused on his career leg. When I asked what issue of vital importance he had about taking the next step forward in his work, he nearly fell off his chair in shock!

He immediately made a meaningful connection. He explained how he had originally studied law because he loved justice. Unfortunately, he had become such a good criminal barrister, that he could get most of his defendants off the hook – even when he secretly believed they might be guilty. So his love for justice, one of his deepest values, had come into conflict with his need to earn a living for his family. Although he had been vaguely aware of this conflict for years, he had not faced it. This all made sense. He felt greatly relieved to think that the lymphoma hadn't come out of the blue. It wasn't random chance. So he felt empowered to make a different choice and resolve this conflict. After some consideration, he decided never to return to the bar and took up a new profession instead. Relieved of the conflict and inner stress, his inner healing felt complete and his lymphoma never returned.

> '*There is some soul of goodness in things evil,*
> *would men observingly distill it out.*'
> William Shakespeare, *Henry V*

Secondary gains

Sometimes the clue lies in what is happening as a result of the illness. Receiving care, attention, sympathy or some other type of reward may indicate an underlying need to be nurtured. Some people stoically continue to carry on, struggling to do everything as usual, but in great pain or discomfort. Perhaps there is something they are trying to prove. Could there be side benefits from having the problem? Perhaps there is something that gets to be avoided.

Always search for such interpretations with great compassion, when you feel most resourceful, open, willing, and curious. When you are highly stressed, there's less opportunity for positive reflection. There's no point in searching for such interpretations and meanings unless it's possible to continue the process and work toward resolution. Avoid confusing responsibility with being to blame. This merely adds guilt on top of the suffering.

If you are curious to know what your body wants to tell you, meditate on what the symptoms could mean. The answers may seem bizarre at first, but pay attention to whatever associations come up. Look for what could be gained or what new opportunity could be opening up. Wonder to yourself: in what ways could this problem intend you to grow or develop?

....

EXERCISE
How to discover the message of a symptom

Label: *Break the 'label' given to an illness down into more specific symptoms. For example, a headache: where exactly do you feel pain? Tumor: where are cells excessively multiplying? Inflammation: what tissue is swollen, red, and angry? Infection: where have lowered defenses allowed invasion by bacteria or viruses? Malfunction: what kind precisely?*

Location: *Where is each symptom located precisely? For example, rashes might appear in different places on the body; each location may have a different meaning. Note which side of the body, left or right. What other meanings or memories do you associate with that area of the body?*

Activity of that body part: *What action has been brought to a halt? What have you been stopped from doing? Why do you want to avoid doing that? Make a list of all the possible reasons and inner conflicts you feel about the activity.*

Secondary benefits: *What do you get as a result of this? How has this benefitted you? What are you gaining? (Attention? Sympathy? Care? Love?)*

Negative gains: *What do you get to avoid? Where do you not have to show up? What do you no longer have to do? In what ways do you get to hide?*

Proof: *What does this prove? What do you get to be right about? Are you stoically carrying on, struggling to do everything as usual, but in so much pain or discomfort that all the enjoyment has gone? (Perhaps proving what a hero you are?)*

Others: *Who might be the target of this unconscious message? Who else in the present or in the past might be associated with this issue? Is it about revenge? Or could sharing the same problem be a way of expressing loyalty with that person?*

Growth: *In what way does this problem cause you to grow? How does this disability develop you in other ways? What are you forced to let go of in order to progress? Who do you need to forgive? What are you being called to do?*

'Do not ask Spirit to heal the body. Ask rather that Spirit teach you the right perception of the body.'
A Course in Miracles, Anon

A significant turning point in my healing process occurred during one of my debilitating headaches. Labeling the recurring pain as a 'headache' blinded me from being able to identify the underlying cause. Plus, the extreme pain made it very difficult to think clearly. Then my guide asked me, 'Where is the pain located?' There were four different focal points: behind my left eye, the center of my head, in my right jaw, and the right side of my neck. 'What if each one is a separate entity?' he asked. 'Could it be that they each have a different message?' Indeed this turned out to be the case. Lumping them together as one 'headache' had previously prevented me from discovering that each one had something different to say. Although they seemed to be working together in a coalition, by exploring each one separately, the messages were more precisely identified, understood, and resolved. The headaches diminished.

Once you know the message of your symptoms, the next step will be to find a meaningful answer that resolves the problem being expressed. You will find guidance for doing this in later chapters. The resolution usually requires making new choices, more in line with who you are and with your purpose. It's the conscious mind, the intellect, the ego, and the old memories, which tend to clutter the mind.

Intuiting your purpose

Take a moment to contemplate all the messages your symptoms have been sending you. What does your body-mind want you to do? How would it like you to be different? What would you like to change? Close your eyes for a moment and gently contemplate what it would be like to have things the way you want them to be. How does it feel? Imagine being fully healed. What does that allow you to do? And when you have achieved that fully and completely, what do you get then? What would that allow you to do? Does this fit with who you came into this world to be? What else would you like to experience?

Your answers may reveal many aspects of your purpose. You may find that you have more than one purpose. What is truly important to you? As the author Steve Covey advises in his classic book *The 7 Habits of Highly Effective People*, just imagine your funeral: what do you want people to be saying about you? How do you want to be remembered? What legacy or contribution makes you feel proud? What will really matter after you have left this planet?

Your true purpose is about what you love to do most. Your purpose gives your life meaning, makes you feel worthwhile, brings a sense of fulfillment, and allows you to live with passion. When you discover your purpose, you will recognize it instantly because it will bring a lump into your throat. It answers the question 'What am I here for?' Living a life of purpose means being in tune with your inner self, making everything you do a spiritual experience.

> 'To laugh often and much; to win the respect of intelligent people and the affection of children…
> to leave the world a better place… to know even one life has breathed easier because you have lived. This is to have succeeded.'
> Ralph Waldo Emerson

The benefit of knowing what you value, what's important to you and how you frame your purpose is well worth investing some time to explore. Pose your questions to your mind each night and wait for the answers to show. When you have clarity of purpose, you will feel more centered, aligned, and inspired. There will be less confusion and more ease about making decisions. Having your inner sense of purpose could be the most important factor of being truly resilient.

ACID TEST QUESTION
How can you tell if you've identified your true purpose?

You will feel motivated, full of determination and perseverance. There will be a sense that you are okay no matter what happens and that giving your best is what counts. You may notice that you choose more positive thoughts and spend more time in the present moment of now. You feel curious and comfortable not knowing all the answers.

Spiritual masters throughout the ages have taught various ways to know oneself: look within, meditate and still the mind. To find a new meaning for your illness and your life means rising above the chatter of everyday thoughts, reasons, internal conflicts, worries, and other negative emotions. Allow your sense of purpose to guide you to find new ways to resolve any problem.

When you know your purpose, you can find new ways to express it, or give it in everything you do. Wherever you go, whomever you are with, whatever you are doing, even the smallest things can demonstrate your purpose. This means everything you do will feel fulfilling. Your purpose may be small, simple, profound, huge, challenging or highly spiritual. Your purpose will make you unstoppable. It will give your life more meaning and increase trust and faith. Becoming aligned with your purpose raises your level of courage, vitality and energy for everything you want to achieve. Living your purpose raises your level of resilience in the face of any crisis.

Key points

▶ People experience problems because they are out of rapport with their unconscious minds.

▶ Emotions trigger the release of hormones throughout the body causing all kinds of chemical and physical changes.

▶ Mindfulness means learning to pay attention to your thoughts.

▶ The conscious and unconscious mind use the same brain cells.

▶ Focus on deep breathing to calm your mind.

▶ Just as you can trust your body to heal small things like a cut finger, you can trust your body to heal bigger problems too.

▶ Symptoms express different metaphorical meanings according to location, the role a part performs, what no longer functions.

▶ Living a life of purpose means being in tune with your inner self, making everything you do more meaningful.

....

Choice Thoughts

I thank the challenges that make me grow.

A small change in thinking has profound effects.

I can do this. I am safe, calm, and relaxed.

The faster I refocus my thoughts, the better I cope.

I trust the normal, natural process of healing.

Knowing my purpose makes me unstoppable.

I am curious about how this will unfold

Chapter 5

How Does Thinking Create Stress?

When life doesn't go according to plan, feeling upset is a common reaction. Disappointment, failure, major upheaval, catastrophe, an ominous diagnosis, loss or trauma usually propels people into a mixture of negative emotions and stress. It feels like the problem caused the stress. The temptation is to jump straight into trying to fix it. That feels better than descending into despair. So proactive people rush into doing something without much thought. Rising to the challenge, they try to maintain a sense of power and control. Looking for instant solutions seems bold, brave and smart. Their motto is 'Anything is better than doing nothing!' The desire to quickly achieve results leads to a frenzied search for magic pills, preferably with guarantees. Such great determination wins approval from everyone.

Defeatists give up without trying. Believing any effort to be futile, they wallow in feelings of gloom. Stressful events make them feel out of control, helpless and powerless. They react with confusion, dissociation and depression, not knowing what to do. Depression is predicted to become the second most common cause of disability by 2020. Many non-specific symptoms such as headaches, tiredness or vague abdominal pains are forms of masked depression. Such pessimists don't believe anything will make a difference. While claiming to be realists, they have merely become convinced by their unreliable perceptions and old habitual thoughts. No space is allowed for new possibilities.

Both types of response ignore the true source of the problem: the unconscious thoughts. Therefore effective and lasting solutions are unlikely. No matter how positively you focus on your desired future, wherever you go your unconscious 'cloud' of thoughts follows. Those habitual thoughts, beliefs, decisions, emotions, and behaviors keep travelling around the old highways in your brain. As they repeat their endless loops it becomes as predictable as the circuits of a racetrack.

Thought clouds

A true hero chooses a different path. First, the hero faces the crisis and hears the call to action. A difficult situation is an invitation to view things differently. The hero responds to the invitation by investigating the issue from a positive perspective, asking better internal questions:

▶ What could be good about this?

▶ What could I learn from this?

▶ How could this help my growth?

▶ What quality is being evolved?

▶ What is not perfect *yet*?

If we ignore the invitation to deal with the crisis, new invites will continue to arrive. Similar problems, more symptoms or other consequences of not facing the issue will arise. Because the same issues will probably resurface to be dealt with, why not face them sooner rather than later? By keeping the focus firmly on the desired future, the hero gains positive energy to explore what is hidden in the cloud of thoughts.

Every journey of exploration will require addressing many challenges. When facing difficult issues, it helps to have loving support, role models, and guides to help you transform whatever may block the path. Perhaps they could read you the questions from some of the exercises. Think about the people who already support you and make sure they know how deeply you appreciate their assistance. Perhaps there are others who could nurture, guide, and sustain you. Consider what will help keep you balanced and motivated to continue when the going gets tough. Notice what you feel willing to do or willing to stop doing.

Connect with your 'Higher Mind' for extra support. Acknowledge the higher guidance and protection that has always been present. Your Higher Mind sees a different perspective of the journey: a perfect path, where the answers lie within. There's trust that the right resourceful solutions will emerge. Instead of rushing to take action, slow down, be calm and reflective in order to access your inner wisdom. As the gurus say, 'Don't just do something, sit there!'

Because old ideas, beliefs, and decisions get embedded in the familiar walls of your comfort zone, they can be easy to overlook and difficult to detect. Your version of reality makes you blind to other perspectives. It takes patience and diligence to discover what has been stored in the unconscious mind. Many people who had happy childhoods and enjoy successful lives feel puzzled and mystified about underlying causes. All their memories and events seem untroubled so they conclude there is nothing to find.

By definition no one can be conscious of what is unconscious. The origin of negative thinking can start from normal, insignificant little events that seem like completely innocent memories. However, these early misperceptions and erroneous conclusions lead to a subsequent chain of negative deductions, thoughts, and feelings later on. Because these were just mistakes, it's possible to unravel this thought process and make new and better decisions.

'There are two mistakes one can make along the road to truth: not going all the way, and not starting.'
Buddha

It is never too late to have a happy childhood

A recent client had to deal with a series of small dramas including money worries, copious application forms, and a possible house move. At the time, she noticed a persistent ache in her kidneys and tightness in her chest and throat that didn't seem coincidental. Instead of overlooking these messages from her body, she decided to explore how these body sensations linked to her chronic pattern of stress. To her surprise, the search took her all the way back to the panic she had felt just after her birth. Of course, she didn't consciously remember her birth. She imagined what it was like by visualization.

Visualizing what her life might have been like as a newborn baby, she imagined feeling like a little mole, with closed eyes and a wrinkly nose. Lying on a blanket alone and scared, she felt ignored, isolated, and unimportant. Where was her mother? During these first moments of life, her panic led to several unconscious judgments: she couldn't trust her mother to be there for her. Therefore life would be lonely, she'd have to fend for herself. Nor could she expect much from anyone else and so she had no choice but to become totally independent and do everything on her own. Life would be full of hard work. She didn't feel happy to be here! Whether or not her birth memory was real, all these fantasies spontaneously emerged from her unconscious imagination.

This odd visualization seemed to explain why she later spent her childhood immersed in books, miserable, despairing, and often crying for no reason. Her relationship with her mother was particularly troublesome. Indeed, as she grew up repeating her unconscious thought patterns, life did seem tough. Too much overwork, rocky relationships, and an unhealthy lifestyle added to being very depressed. Counseling and medication didn't help much. Despite her life taking a turn for the better at age 37, she then received an unwelcome surprise: a diagnosis of multiple sclerosis.

What an ironic coincidence that her drive to be totally independent was now challenged by a disease that carried the risk of her becoming totally dependent. It seemed that those early negative ideas had built strong foundations in her brain. Those original perceptions had established the walls of her uncomfortable comfort zone. But a thought structure built on top of such mistakes and flimsy deductions actually has no stability. Like a house built on sand, it will sink or tumble down.

In fact the true story of her birth story turned out to be quite different. After trying to have a baby for over four years, her mother had been positively thrilled and delighted to have her first daughter. But giving birth had exhausted her and throughout the ordeal she felt panicky about losing this precious baby. She herself had been adopted and lacked natural mothering skills. She didn't know how to connect or bond with her baby daughter. Later she felt quite scared of this child who seemed impossible to please.

Clearly the 'mole's' negative judgments about the birth experience needed to be updated! Luckily, she found it easy to correct these old mistaken thoughts. It's never too late to have a happy childhood! Using a gentle process to connect with that part of her mind, she reframed each old judgment and installed positive ideas about how much she has always been loved, wanted, supported, safe, important, and valued. She could ask for help and trust that God always wanted the best for her. Life didn't have to be a struggle. She could stop worrying, relax and enjoy the moment. Perhaps it was no coincidence that shortly after changing these thoughts, an extraordinary event occurred: her mother rang her just for a friendly chat.

*'Miracles are natural. When they do not
occur something has gone wrong.'*
A Course in Miracles, Anon

This story points out the crucial distinction to make between conscious and unconscious decisions. Most people have completely forgotten what was programmed into their brains at a very young age. You can intuit this early input by examining the current events. Just carefully observe what's happening now. The present state of affairs usually reflects the early dynamics. In some way, when things haven't gone according to plan it could be an invitation to explore more deeply. Accept the opportunity to make better choices and develop new understanding. Many deep change processes or therapeutic techniques currently available can be of great assistance. Do seek expert help.

Seeing without eyes

Scientists have no way to explain where consciousness really comes from or what it is. Nor have they been able to verify where memory is stored. There are theories that try to explain consciousness as a side effect of neuropeptides, or the quantum coherence of tiny microtubules found in nerve cells, or something to do with chaos and complexity theory, but none of these ideas actually explain how brain activity creates the experience of consciousness. Many of these theories just try to squash consciousness into the existing model of a material world where the body is regarded as a machine.

Most people confuse sensory awareness with consciousness but they are not the same. What you think, decide and do is driven by the unconscious part of your mind. There's a part of the unconscious that receives much more information than what your eyes, ears, mouth, nose, or skin can sense. In the documentary *The Living Matrix* a study done by The Institute of Noetic Science revealed very surprising results. After wiring up volunteers to measure the responses from the brain and specific parts of the body, they had the volunteers view a computer screen. The computer randomly selected images that were either full of peace and joy, or very threatening and fearful. To everyone's amazement, the electrodes measuring the body showed a response to the picture *before* the image appeared on the screen. Even more surprising, it was the heart that responded with emotions appropriate to each picture, not the brain. So the heart somehow knows what's about to happen in your environment, before the eyes and brain have time to construct any images.[1]

The conscious and the unconscious mind use the same brain cells so it's possible to access the unconscious through keen observation. Just notice and listen to your mind. Even the smallest feelings of being attracted or repelled can give you valuable clues. Listen to your dissatisfactions. What you don't like is just as important as what you do like. Those things that currently make you feel miserable simultaneously reveal what you want instead. Ask yourself what that might be. Instead of suppressing your misery with food, drink, pills, phone, TV, playing computer games, or over-exercising listen to what your mind wants to say. What needs to change in your life? For example, if your work makes you miserable:

‣ What would you really like to do with your time?

‣ What would you do if you were sure you would never fail?

▶ What would you do if you could be sure you would succeed?

▶ What would you continue to do even if you were not paid?

Your purpose is not your job, your fame, or how much money you earn. If you listen to your heart, it knows your true purpose. Your heart isn't concerned with current trends and cultural norms. Your heart knows what you came to do. Maybe what you really need is more courage to be who you came to be, more self-love to accept yourself just as you are. Perhaps you already do this in many ways. If you asked your heart what is most important to you, what would it say about your purpose in life?

▶ What would make you feel more vibrantly alive?

▶ What would happen if you enlarged upon this?

▶ What would happen if you lived your purpose?

The art of mindfulness

Mindfulness begins with awareness, being totally present, being totally in the 'Now' as spiritual masters have recommended throughout time. How much time do you actually spend attuned to all your senses, focused on what's going on in the here and now? How quickly does your mind slip into thinking about the past, making judgments, pre-conceptions, projections, opinions, conclusions, and beliefs? How much time do you spend worrying and projecting these on the future? Being truly responsible requires the ability to discipline your thoughts, to stop unhelpful thinking in its tracks. All it takes is a little practice to be mindful. Life can only be lived one moment at a time no matter how enjoyable or how awful. Remember you only have to deal with this moment right now. You will never get to experience this moment again. How precious is that? Being 100 percent present and mindful allows your intuition and healing energy to flow.

How to enhance mindfulness

▶ Pay attention to what is happening in each moment.

▶ Sit with the uncertainty and discomfort of not knowing.

▶ Keep yourself out of the picture; avoid jumping into action.

▶ Be comfortable with confusion and clarity will show itself.

▶ Trust in the process; avoid being attached to the outcome.

▶ Foster a sense of just being: be right here, right now, in this moment.

The more energy we put into trying to change or heal something, the more we reinforce the reality of the problem. This paradox exists because we must have fully accepted the problem as real before even thinking of trying to fix it. Now the problem becomes how can we want to heal and at the same time, let go of the desire to heal? How can we want things to change yet put up with the way things are now? How can we accept what we most want to get rid of? In order to solve this paradox we must trust in the process.

> '*Better to light a candle than to curse the darkness.*'
> Chinese proverb

At the beginning of my healing journey I found it difficult to identify any mental or emotional cause associated with my tumor. It seemed like a mystery because I had no idea, no awareness of any reason or negative trauma in my past. Practicing mindfulness helped to increase my awareness and discover a hidden cause. One day I remembered a vague memory from my early childhood, about my mother being quite unwell, grumpy, and distracted by pain due to a series of different illnesses. Although there were no traumatic memories, there were too few good memories. Consequently my child mind made formative decisions about how little fun it was to be a mother, run a house, and look after babies. These thoughts must have taken root and branched out, influencing many other decisions. Years later my conscious awareness focused entirely on my desire to have children. Meanwhile the hidden negative ideas about motherhood silently created strong resistance and deep internal conflict about having children. So was it just coincidence that my body chose to grow a tumor making me infertile?

Three responses to trauma

When people feel like victims, they commonly suffer because their beliefs about the world get shattered. They suffer from three sources of distress: fear of their vulnerability, doubt about the world being meaningful, and being unable to hold a positive view of oneself or the future. Some will become dispirited; some will get their lives back to normal. The ones who fare best are those who view the experience as defining their life and giving them strength.[2] When bad things happen to good people, why do some choose to give up while others persevere? What motivates those who choose to make the experience about learning, growing, becoming stronger, and giving? Why do others continue to feel like victims and choose upset, fear, anger, or stress?

People who survive major challenges – illness, war, accident, loss, or repeated failure – see those events as major turning points of their lives. They redefine who they are, what they do, and why they do it, in the most positive and humble way. Such people persevere, trusting and having faith that whatever their journey entails, they will prevail in the end and reach the desired destination, even if it looks a bit different from what they originally envisioned. They let go of their plan and begin to trust, taking each moment one at a time. They have gratitude for the wonder of the experience itself. They have learned to say 'yes' to life with love, openness, happiness, and the spirit of giving.

> *'There is no value in life except what you choose to place upon it and no happiness in any place except what you bring to it yourself.'*
> Henry David Thoreau

Becoming a true hero

What if you presuppose there could be a positive purpose associated with your problem? You could do your best to interpret the metaphoric messages and symptoms for clues, and be open and willing to learn whatever lessons might be involved. Harboring thoughts that your body has let you down or you are at the mercy of some evil fate or a saboteur obstructs your way leads to feeling powerless and losing trust. Illness doesn't get created overnight. Stress originates from complex and multiple causes: mental, emotional, and physical. It takes years of repetitive stress, negative thinking and poor habits to have an impact on the immune system.

Therefore it is rare for one simple change, one shift of thinking or one affirmation to turn the whole process around. There may be many layers, many different aspects that need to be addressed.

When habitual thoughts have traveled down the same route for many years, they create three-lane highways in the brain. That's why people often react before thinking. Just a word, a look, a voice tone, or some other small thing can trigger a lightning-fast response. Don't be surprised if some of these old issues resurface. What has remained hidden and unresolved until now may feel a little uncomfortable. In order to avoid the old repetitive routes, the brain needs practice: consistent, congruent, compassionate mindfulness. To identify the triggers that led to those thoughts in the past helps avoid falling into those traps again. First choose how you would like to respond instead. Remember and trust you can always find a way through, no matter how much your resolve may be tested.

Three sources of stress

A healing journey requires making better choices and having better responses to everything that happens in your environment. When obstacles block the path, the difference that makes the real difference is how you respond. Obstacles come from three different sources of stress: external, intimate, and internal. Each source of stress requires different kinds of healing.

The 'external' sources of stress that block the path are the most obvious: job issues, money issues, body symptoms, relationship or family problems. These will require more physical solutions, treatments, or new decisions. 'Intimate' sources may be more devastating, as these come from people who may mean to be supportive, who appear to be helping, but who actually create obstacles by getting in the way. Some helpers try to take control, obstruct your decisions, or impede your progress. This source of stress requires solving complex relationship problems. However, the most dangerous are the 'internal' sources: your old personal beliefs, what has been accepted as true in the past, and what you believe is possible or impossible. Luckily you have the power to change these habitual thought patterns immediately. Although this book deals mainly with the internal sources of stress, you may need to address the other sources too.[3]

'Faith in oneself is the best and safest course.'
Michelangelo

Good things can come of this

People benefit most by learning about themselves as a result of struggling with crisis, illness, hardship, or loss. It may be a cliché you hate but there's truth in the old proverb: 'Every cloud has a silver lining.' Many report that their relationships deepen, or that they finally get the courage to leave a dysfunctional relationship. Some discover strengths they never knew they had. Some gain a heightened sense of spirituality and a greater appreciation for the value of life. You might find it useful to write down your daily thoughts in a private journal, partly to download what is on your mind and partly as a process of self-discovery. The objective is to identify whatever helps to enhance your sense of meaning. Many people find that meditation and spiritual practice help to foster resilience.

Suffering makes people ask different questions. What does suffering want to teach you? Healing takes place after you find your deep answers from within. A significant inner shift occurs when you fully own the solution. In a sense that is the moment of true healing. The physical improvements follow more slowly and reflect the new inner state when the thoughts remain consistent over time. If your symptoms gave you a message, what would you be willing to do? If you stood up for what is most important to you, and started living your purpose, how would that fulfill your values? Perhaps suffering is not obligatory.

ACID TEST QUESTION
How can you tell if your thoughts are based on truth or unconscious fantasies?

Simple, just notice how you feel. If your inner state feels truly peaceful, happy, at ease, creative, grounded, and balanced then your predominant thoughts hold truth. If you feel irritated, frustrated, anxious, worried, disappointed, depressed, jealous, envious, or guilty then your thoughts reflect old unconscious mistakes.

No matter how justified the argument or how much evidence can be piled up, a negative story doesn't have to produce a matching negative state. Once those events get fully processed, resolved, forgiven, and put to rest, the same type of event produces feelings of compassion and peace. That doesn't mean bad behavior should be condoned or negative events never happened. The healed perspective is what counts. Our negative feelings serve an incredibly important purpose; they tell us immediately when our thinking has gone off course. We just need to identify which thoughts might be responsible and what we're willing to change.

> *'I have spent most of my life worrying*
> *about things that have never happened.'*
> Mark Twain

Old stories, decisions, beliefs, and convictions from the past cause confusion and cloud the thinking. We must not be distracted or deterred. Make clarity and inner peace the goal. The need to feel in control and have guaranteed results can hold us back. Don't expect to know the answers in advance. If it were that easy, there wouldn't be a problem. Commit to crossing thresholds avoided in the past.

Instead of thinking gloom and doom thoughts, why not commit to making a new choice? If what we focus on is what we get then it's worth training our minds to focus on a positive future. To really stretch our thinking, why not start with pretending everything is just the way we want it. Just suppose there could be a positive purpose for events to be exactly as they are right now. How could this be a good thing to have happened? What new options become available? In what ways do we get to learn, become stronger, and more resilient? Do these answers bring increased energy and motivation, a can-do attitude, more determination, more persistence, and lots more choices? When we exercise the mindfulness to grow from challenges, future hardships become tolerable.

What if you stopped working on your weaknesses, and started appreciating your unique talents and strengths? What if you stopped trying to fix yourself, and started accepting and nurturing your true identity? What if you stopped squeezing yourself into conventional expectations, and started stretching the boundaries to grow into who you've always wanted to become? Every choice you make, everything you accept as true will begin to shape your new reality.

Key points

▶ Most of what you think, feel, decide, and do is driven by the unconscious part of your mind.

▶ Mindfulness begins with such awareness, being totally present, being totally in the 'now.'

▶ The more energy you put into trying to get anything to change, the more you reinforce the reality of the problem.

▶ People who survive major challenges choose to see those events as major turning points of their lives.

▶ It takes years of repetitive stress, negative thinking, and poor habits to have an impact on the immune system.

▶ Avoiding old thought highways needs practice: consistent, congruent, compassionate mindfulness.

▶ A negative story doesn't have to produce a matching negative state.

▶ Negative feelings serve an incredibly important purpose; they tell you immediately when your thinking has gone off course

....

Choice Thoughts

I trust the best resourceful solutions will emerge.

I can sit with the uncertainty and discomfort of not knowing.

My life can only be lived one moment at a time.

I have gratitude for the wonder of the experience itself.

I trust in the process and stay unattached to the outcome.

I am saying 'yes' to life with love, openness, and happiness.

My purpose brings me clarity and inner peace.

Chapter 6

How to Weather a Virtual Storm

Negative thoughts behave like virtual storms in our unconscious minds. Without due care and attention, these storms whirl around creating havoc throughout our system. However, if we examine the mistakes and misperceptions at the basis of each thought, they evaporate. This means we need to become aware of our negative responses long enough to obtain the information we need.

Collect these thoughts simply by noticing every little idea or reaction you have around a specific issue. Look at what you feel less than happy about. Go beyond your everyday dissociated state of being okay, cool, and competent. Look into the small irritations, any unexplainable loss of energy, or feeling a bit low. Explore any ideas that might be connected. Where do they come from, what thoughts seem related? Have you been trying to achieve something that never happens? Have you ever caught yourself thinking 'life was supposed to be different'? Ask yourself what life should have been like and check whether those expectations were realistic. Common everyday thoughts reflect a mirror image of deeper inner

....

beliefs hidden within. Pay attention to the little thoughts because they reveal what needs to be reassessed.

> *'The thought manifests as the word, the word manifests as the deed, the deed develops into habit, and habit hardens into character. So watch the thought and its ways with care. And let it spring from love, born out of concern for all beings.'*
> Buddha

Catch unconscious negative thoughts

During my healing journey I would always wake up enjoying a few moments of feeling totally okay, peaceful, and relaxed. Then as my brainwaves switched into gear, a black cloud of thoughts descended to obscure all those good feelings. This cloud of thoughts reminded me that I still had to deal with a brain tumor. Unfortunately not only didn't I know what had caused the tumor, I also had no idea what would help. Of course this led to worry, confusion, and more negative thoughts about being a failure. Although this kind of thinking seemed stressful, it held all the clues.

The body is not a machine, thoughts are not solid objects, and healing is not purely physical. We need to look beyond the physical and let go of rigid ideas. If you are interested there are new scientific theories that explain how the body works, from the cells down to the energy particles within the 'Field.' But understanding everything about science is unnecessary in order to heal. What is important to know is that conscious and unconscious thoughts supply the energy that drives the process we experience as reality. Problems occur when thoughts set in motion long ago still govern what appears to be real today. Every thought radiates energy that vibrates out into the universe. Whatever resonates with that frequency comes vibrating back to the senses. Because this resonance seems to verify the thought, the brain recognizes and accepts it as fact. It is like the brain says, 'See, I told you so!' Just like searching for red convertibles, it starts seeing them everywhere. But millions of other frequencies and choices are always available as alternatives. Therefore everyone's version of reality will be different.

Repetitive stress spirals create different emotional energy fields, which we experience as moods. Stress thoughts gather together with like-minded ideas and feelings. Each spiral joins forces with other similar ideas, beliefs, memories and emotions to build 'thought clouds' that fog the brain. While it might have been possible to deal with each thought separately, when they all gang up together the combined effect is overpowering.

Thoughts gather into clouds

Long before a serious illness has been diagnosed, the thought cloud will have escalated into a virtual storm. Unprocessed emotions create an internal howling gale, whipping up stress hormones and sweeping through the body. Such a tornado of beliefs, conflicts, self-attack, and internal turmoil can feel completely overwhelming. The difficulty of confronting the full fury of such a storm explains why few have the courage to examine, identify, or question any of those original thoughts. Yet that is precisely what needs to be done.

As quickly as weather can change, these negative thoughts can evaporate. After the clouds get blown away, the blue sky and sunshine above are revealed. Learn how to blow away the mistakes and lies of old outmoded thoughts, and choose to rediscover the truth. Remember you have the choice to think differently and your true identity will be revealed. Celebrate your uniqueness and magnificence and step back into your power.

'*Though this be madness, yet there is method in't.*'
William Shakespeare, *Hamlet*

A thought cloud of panic

With a little awareness and observation, it's easy to collect the different elements that make up a thought cloud. Perhaps you may have already noticed how one problem tends to link with another. Negative loops, internal conflicts, and 'double binds' combine their dizzy energy to swirl you round and leave you confused and bewildered. A good example is the story of a very successful sales director who could not understand why he had suffered three debilitating panic attacks during the last 10 years. He hadn't been able to identify the cause and so he worried that another one could spring on him at any time. As he told his story several key phrases stood out, revealing his major issues. Gradually a very complex thought cloud emerged out of the tangle of his conflicting thoughts.

At first his three panic attacks all sounded quite different. The first one occurred quite understandably when he got 'trapped' in a totally unsuitable job, and then allowed his confidence to be undermined. The stress of 'not feeling good enough' led to panic about failing. The reason he hated feeling trapped was because his most important value was freedom. This first panic attack left him in a depression that lasted for more than a year.

The second incident also sounded totally understandable. After the birth of his son, he and his wife didn't budget properly and overspent until their debt spiraled out of control. This time he beat himself up for being incompetent, until he felt so much panic he could barely function. Again he felt 'not good enough' and 'trapped.' Although it took a few years as well as medication, he eventually pulled himself out of the panic and gradually paid off the enormous debt.

However, the third depression worried him the most. When this panic hit, he felt like he had been suddenly spiraled down a 'mine shaft' of anxiety and depression for no reason. It made no sense. Everything in his life was going superbly well. The earlier debt had all been paid back, his kids were growing up, he had lots of fulfilling work, and money was flowing in. Small stresses, like arguing with his wife a little bit and possibly drinking too much, didn't explain

....

why he suddenly took a dive. This time the intense panic lasted four months before it disappeared just as mysteriously as it had arrived. Consequently he began to fear these attacks because they seemed totally out of his control, beyond reason or logic.

Together we traced the origin of his belief about 'not being good enough' back to when he was a boy. His father, the principal of the local school, was a super sportsman and highly competitive achiever, who always had to win at all costs. He also had to be right about everything too. His young son knew being a winner was the only way to 'get approval.' Unfortunately, despite trying his best to meet these high expectations, the son couldn't match his father's superior performance. To make matters worse his father often helped his son behind the scenes by pulling strings.

Consequently when the boy received prizes, awards, or scholarships, he could never be sure he legitimately 'deserved' them. Fearing that his father might have arranged things in his favor, he felt nothing but embarrassment. The message he got from his father was clear: you are 'only okay if you win.' But because he wasn't sure whether he had earned those prizes 'winning meant nothing.' To make matters worse, even when he did win, he got no praise, no points, and no acknowledgement from his father. He felt terrified of 'letting people down' and mortified if he won, but he had to win to be okay. The collection of thoughts combined to form a whole cloud of negative emotions, double binds, and limiting beliefs.

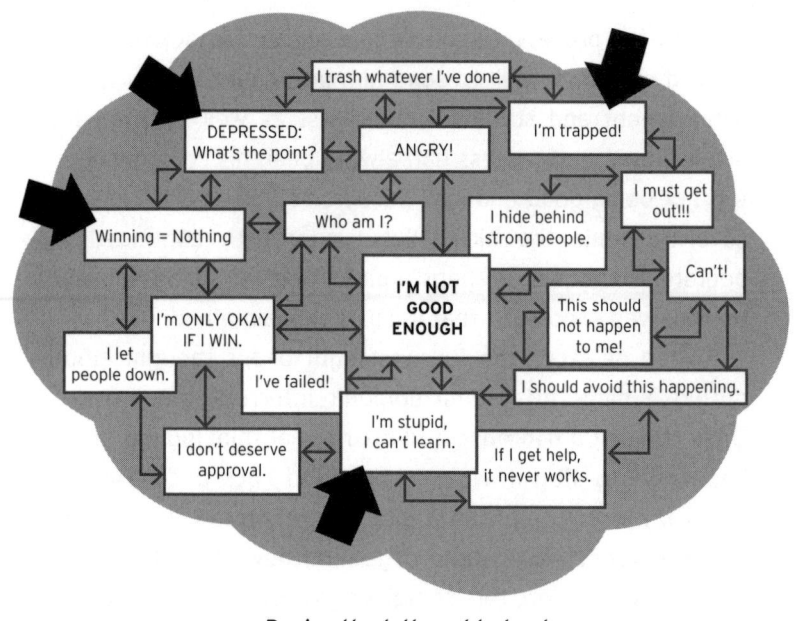

Panic attack thought cloud

Although originally each thought related to different events at different ages, they all interconnected and reappeared during each panic attack. Each thought pushed him in different directions, bouncing him back and forth like the ball in a pinball machine. The pressure to achieve and win drove him to keep trying to meet impossible expectations. But success brought no pleasure, only depression. By trying his best to avoid failure and prove his worth, he lost sight of his true identity and also lost any real sense of satisfaction. So he got little respite from the internal stress.

Over time subsequent behaviors, derogatory self-talk, and associated negative emotions filled the spaces in between the original conflicting thoughts. What a work of art! The thinking strategy of his cloud worked perfectly every time and always produced the same result: panic. Different triggers could start off the process. Of course fear and self-attack thoughts worked extremely well to send him into panic. But curiously achievement and success worked just as well. Striving for achievement and success had always been his compensation for 'not being good enough.' Success served as an elaborate cover-up while the old beliefs underneath continued to operate as triggers. Perhaps a part of him still didn't believe he deserved success or that it could be maintained.

When he faced the full onslaught of his thought cloud during a panic attack, he couldn't interrupt the process. Once the cloud had obscured his normal thinking, he didn't know how to stop it. Now as he stood back and observed the crazy structure of the whole picture, he saw things from a new perspective. Instead of feeling powerless, he began to understand how the combined elements had kept him lost in this old inner fog. He also realized this vaporous cloud of thoughts didn't represent what was real or true. He began to question the validity of these unhelpful ideas and beliefs. He also became more curious to discover the hidden positive elements.

'I have lived on the lip
Of insanity, wanting to know reasons,
Knocking on a door. It opens.
I've been knocking from the inside!'
Rumi

Despite the confusion and stress generated by such a cloud, the origin of each individual thought comes from innocent mistakes of reasoning and errors of perception. Each thought started with positive intentions and values appropriate at the time. For example 'feeling stupid' would not be an issue unless a deeper value for 'being smart' existed as well, so don't be concerned or embarrassed by negative-sounding ideas. By constructing your cloud you will diminish their power and expose them as mistakes. Later the attention will focus on working with one particular thought at a time. This makes it easier to trace the origin, correct the mistakes, and shift the energy. The process may need to be repeated with several thoughts making up the cloud before the real shift occurs.

....

EXERCISE
Construct your thought cloud

What works best is to write down each separate thought on a Post-It note. Quietly contemplate a specific issue. Avoid starting with your biggest issue. Use a less important one to practice on first. Collect the various phrases, beliefs, ideas, etc. by simply listing your most common thoughts or by writing down your story and then underlining key phrases. It's best to do this exercise when you're feeling highly resourceful, cool, calm and collected. Don't try this exercise for the first time when you are right in the middle of turmoil. Without prior practice, and until you know how to reframe each thought, focusing on the negative aspects could temporarily make you feel worse. So it would be very helpful if you have someone objective who can listen to the story and help to collect the phrases with you.

Collect the key phrases and hot emotions used to describe events, as well as habitual sayings, statements of fact, judgments, and beliefs. Pay particular attention to negative self-assessments and blame. With each thought written on a separate Post-it note, you can move them around. Pictures and symbols can also be used to depict complicated ideas. Intuitively arrange all the Post-Its on a sheet of paper. Notice how one thought leads to another and begin linking them to show the direction of the thought process. How does one thought connect to other related thoughts? Include as many as needed until the construction of the cloud starts to build. It isn't important to arrange them perfectly. The real value comes from collecting as many as possible into the cloud where they can be observed from a distance. You can always add to it later.

Particularly look out for areas that loop around to create double binds. What is a double bind? A good example is one of my favorite cartoons by Gary Larsen: a man stands in hell facing two identical doors. Behind him, the devil is prodding his backside with a pitchfork. Over one door it says, 'Damned if you do,' over the other, 'Damned if you don't.' The devil says, 'C'mon, c'mon make up your mind, it's either one or the other!' A simple double bind is a conflict or struggle between equal and opposing ideas, desires, or intentions. It usually feels like a choice between two equally undesirable alternatives. In addition to the difficult choice and the pressure to act, there may also be insurmountable obstacles that create a complete impasse. The complications are as endless as the looping of the thoughts. As one double bind links to another, an impossible tangle of obsessive thinking results.

The thoughts floating around your thought cloud may seem elusive at first. Once you catch a few of the thoughts, listen carefully for associated ideas, behaviors, and language patterns that reveal judgments. Listen for phrases using 'should, shouldn't, must, have to, can't' and anything that sounds punishing or derogatory. Pay particular attention to any phrases that get repeated as 'family rules' or emphasized as 'truths.' Keep adding new thoughts to the cloud until your work of art is as complete as possible. Keep adding new thoughts to the cloud until your work of art is as complete as possible.

Thought cloud focus questions:

◊ *What emotions are associated with that thought?*

◊ *How long has that thought been present – since what age?*

◊ *When did it start: what was the story at the time?*

◊ *What needed to be defended or protected?*

◊ *How did it affect your self-esteem and self-worth?*

◊ *What did you believe would happen in the future?*

Mapping out all your limiting beliefs may make you feel uncomfortable as you become aware of many negative thoughts all at once. Remember they sit inside your mind whether you are aware of them or not. Surely it is better to be aware of what causes stress so you have the opportunity for change. You cannot change what you do not know. By bringing your thought cloud into the light, you will be able to pinpoint exactly what needs to change and where to apply more positive thinking.

Depicting your cloud pulls the thoughts out of your head. Once they are down on paper or laid out on a table, you can stand back and review the whole pattern from a distance. This in itself adds a cool sense of perspective. When you see the whole structure of the cloud and get a sense of how it works, it will never have quite the same power again. The thought cloud is not <u>who</u> you are; it's just a strategy of thinking that used to get stuck.

'You may believe that you are responsible for what you do, but not for what you think. The truth is that you are responsible for what you think, because it is only at this level that you can exercise choice. What you do comes from what you think.'
A Course in Miracles, Anon

A thought cloud rarely seems logical or rational. Don't spend time trying to make sense of it, organize it, modify it, or justify it – yet. Simply appreciate the fabrication of this crazy work of art as it is, and note how predictably well it operates. Notice once a cloud gets triggered, the end result is almost guaranteed. How efficient! Just think if a negative cloud produces such a reliable result, the same must be true of a positive cloud too.

All kinds of problems originate from complex thought clouds. A common mistake of magic-pill thinking is that doing one piece of change work will be enough to heal a difficult problem. After viewing the complexity of a whole cloud, it is obvious why simple approaches don't always work. If only one aspect is addressed, it may have too little impact on the whole cloud. Particularly when the surrounding environment remains full of all the original triggers and negative energy, the cloud may simply reinstate itself. The walls of thoughts can be so robust and well practiced that they resist any change until you find the keystone holding them all together. That could explain why people say they initially feel good after a session, but the positive change doesn't last. Instead of concluding that the therapy was ineffective, consider the complexity of the cloud.

The next thing to do is to identify the triggers that switch on a thought cloud. If these triggers can be avoided, changed, or switched off then the cloud won't click into action. This will reduce stress immediately. Triggers are just habits of response. To change them, however, may require lots of willingness and a little practice. Once you identify the trigger that switches on a particular thought cloud, it will be easy to spot next time it tries to click into action. Instead of collapsing into the chaos, just notice it: 'Oh look, I seem to be doing that thought cloud again.' Later you can focus on making better choices and healing the issues in the cloud, but right now just discover what triggers your cloud into action.

....

EXERCISE
Discover the triggers

With regard to your thought cloud, think about the stressful situations that cause you to feel less than comfortable, happy and at peace. Some classic triggers might be: getting stuck in traffic, dealing with rush-hour crowds, being late, the look on someone's face, a tone of voice, a particular body sensation, a limiting belief, etc. If it helps, replay a recent stressful event in your mind and see if you can answer the following questions.

◊ **Identify the trigger:** What is the very first thing you are aware of that initiates or starts the stress?

◊ **Behavior:** What do you think? What do you say? How do you behave? What do you do? (For example, loud voice, curse, stonewall, retreat, etc.).

◊ **Physical effects:** What happens in your body? (For example, tension, red face, increased heart rate, rashes, pain, other symptoms, etc.).

◊ **Emotion:** What emotions accompany the thoughts and beliefs? (For example, anger, fear, sadness, guilt, etc.).

◊ **Thoughts:** What chain of thoughts follows? Can you recall the sequence of thoughts? What movies (of the past or future) do you run?

◊ **Meanings:** What will all this mean or what effects do you expect will happen as a result? What do you predict will occur?

Once you have identified some of the main triggers that switch on your cloud, you can brainstorm possible ways to avoid them. If you can remove the trigger from your environment, or move yourself away from the trigger, this will obviously reduce the number of times you experience the cloud. Although this won't heal the issues involved, it will give you a rest. So some obvious examples with regard to the above suggestions might be: change your commuting times, work flexible hours, *leave earlier, have fewer meetings with unpleasant people, wear earplugs, do whatever you can to help your body feel more comfortable (better diet, more rest, more exercise, specific treatments, etc.).*

....

'We are what we repeatedly do.
Excellence, then, is not an act but a habit.'
Aristotle

Lack of self-worth

In this example the story began with issues to do with food, but ended up with issues about self-worth. Notice the three main triggers in the arrows: lack of trust, loneliness, and time pressure. All the beliefs, decisions, and negative feelings kept the cloud spinning, with loops of energy going around and around keeping it stuck. The way one thought linked to another almost made sense, but the overall cloud seemed quite illogical. Despite all evidence of success, this woman trashed herself as a complete failure, because she was convinced she wasn't good enough. Having suffered many disappointments in personal relationships, her hopes were now dashed. Her dreams, fantasies, and expectations of happiness seemed out of reach. Despite doing lots of self-improvement work, her self-esteem remained low. In fact her constant efforts to lose weight, be more attractive, and improve herself reinforced the negative self-assessment and kept the dynamic of the cloud firmly in place.

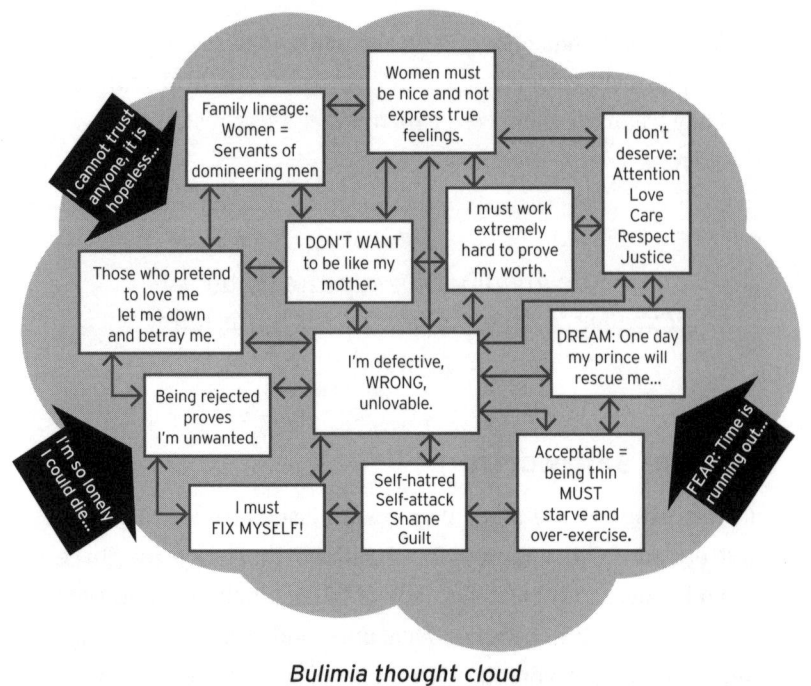

Bulimia thought cloud

Almost any of the negative thoughts in this cloud could trigger the never-ending loops, producing low energy, depression, and enough confusion to drive her suppression strategy. Her stress found an outlet in habitual behaviors around food. Unfortunately overeating provided only temporary relief. Despite the self-punishment of starvation her yo-yo diet caused more weight gain, leading to more self-hatred. Somehow the focus needed to be taken away from food, diets, exercise, and all attempts to *look* acceptable. Her energy needed to move toward a healthy self-concept: being totally okay, acceptable, lovable, and knowing her true self-worth. Only then could attempts to improve diet and fitness be free from the sense of punishment. True self-worth needed to include taking care of her body out of self-love, rather than self-hatred.

Whether you want to heal a specific illness, build a lucrative career, or find the perfect partner, it helps to fully understand the underlying dynamics in your thought cloud. This will also help explain what holds you back and where these unhelpful thoughts originated. Instead of feeling helpless and out of control, you can begin to understand what to do. Most people discover positive intentions within the stories that created their clouds. In some way the original decisions and beliefs were an attempt to protect, value, or stand up for something important. However, these original decisions may have long outlived their usefulness.

*'Life has a bright side and a dark side,
for the world of relativity is composed of
light and shadows. If you permit your thoughts
to dwell on evil, you yourself will become ugly.
Look only for the good in everything so you
absorb the quality of beauty.'*
Paramahansa Yogananda

No matter what kind of crisis you may be facing, you can learn a lot from understanding the deeper dynamics. The benefits come from creating new meaning and allowing the whole cloud to become a part of your evolution. The details and decisions of the events provide clues to discovering what underlying ideas and beliefs may have been the source. Perhaps some of your old values may need to be reassessed. If you opened up these opportunities for growth and change, and stepped more fully into your power, what is the worst that could happen?

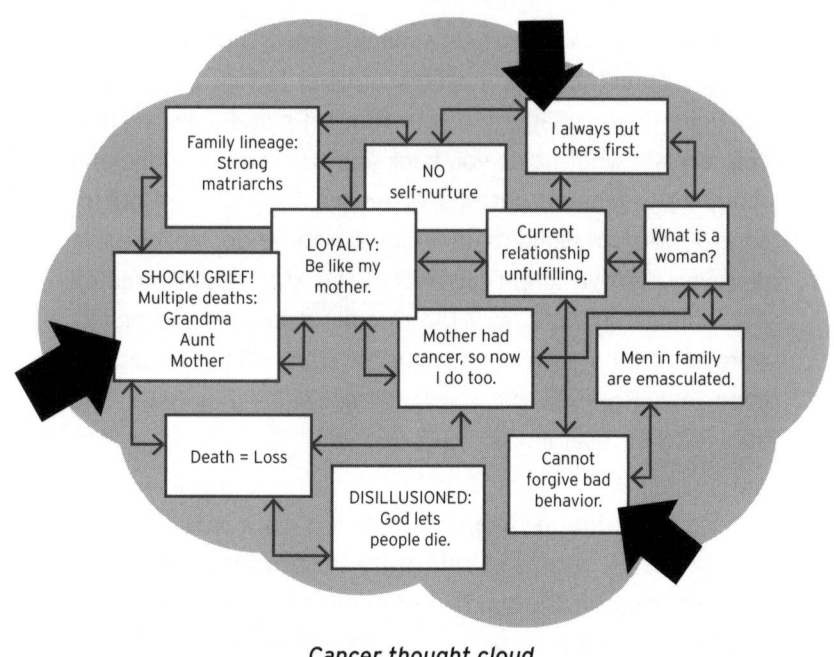

Cancer thought cloud

Suppressed beliefs

The lady in this story demonstrated a common tendency of people who develop cancer: she held high levels of anxiety yet suppressed all her worries, pretending everything was fine. However many research studies indicate that positive improvements in cancer patients can be achieved simply by dealing with the underlying stress, and so her willingness to deal with her cloud represented a big step forward. Unfortunately her sweet, kind and gentle exterior nature got in the way. The symptoms of cancer in the breast and spine pointed the exploration toward issues of self-nurturing, support, and ancestors.

Breast cancer had affected at least three generations in her family. So on the surface that seems to support the genetic link argument. However the old ideas about genes causing cancer completely ignored the associated beliefs, values, and behaviors of those families. In this case the beliefs and values of this long lineage of very strong women could not be ignored. The women held all the power and controlled every decision about family life and finances. These wives were so strong that as a result their mates became emasculated and provided little support. These powerful women decreed rules about loyalty and how women should behave, like 'put others first.' However, when these women practiced giving to others first, they never had time to self-nurture. Without giving enough attention to their needs, their self-value diminished. Indeed in this family the rules overemphasized caring for each other. This altruism probably led to some confusion about identity and self-worth.

Cancer often follows an intense shock, such as loss or the death of someone close. After experiencing the recent shock of losing both her aunt and her mother, she suffered significant spiritual disillusionment. She longed to be like her mother, but this loss of her cherished role model diminished her sense of self. Remember the immune system depends on being able to identify what belongs inside us and what does not. The white blood cells have to differentiate the cells that match our identity from the aberrant cancer cells that don't match and should be removed. Could her white blood cells have been confused about her identity? Her cloud of thoughts indicated that redefining her sense of who she was, especially her identity as a woman, could be a key healing issue.

Hot spots in your cloud

Rather than dwell too long gazing at a thought cloud, it is better to look at it from afar and then put it away. To view it from a distance allows you to separate yourself from the mistaken cloud of ideas and beliefs that don't represent your true identity. Avoid judging it harshly. Appreciate that each concept was once the best thought you could have had, with the best intention you could come up with at the time. Be curious about how the whole cloud may provide important motivation for your learning, understanding and evolution.

The next step is to identify the key factors: the hot spots. Look for the negative beliefs that stand out, the primary issues, internal conflicts, and double binds. Where does the energy get most stuck? Which statement holds the most important value? Which negative emotions keep surfacing? It may be unnecessary to address every aspect. Intuitively assess the cloud to discover where to start the healing. Every shift of thinking will help, so no effort is wasted. Here are some questions to help identify the hot spots that need the most attention.

EXERCISE
Questions to identify the key elements

◊   *Where is the emphasis, the hottest energy loop?*

◊   *What repetitive emotions accompany each statement?*

◊   *What decisions were made, and at what age?*

◊   *What other decisions or choices were made?*

◊   *What is believed and accepted as true?*

◊   *What are the self-judgments in the internal dialogue?*

◊　　*Where are there obvious internal conflicts?*

◊　　*Where are there double binds – no-win situations?*

◊　　*What is believed about possibility and capability?*

◊　　*What is deeply desired and probably blocked?*

◊　　*What is the belief about what is deserved?*

◊　　*What important role does time play in this?*

....

ACID TEST QUESTION
How do you know you have collected all the important elements of your cloud?

Although it may not feel entirely comfortable, somehow it will seem to make sense. It should feel familiar. You will start making new connections and possibly have some old memories resurface. There may also be a sense of relief knowing the reasons and dynamics behind a particular problem. As you start to shift your thinking, you may already start feeling more relaxed and in control. Please remember to be extremely compassionate toward everything you discover in your cloud. Every belief and thought began with positive intentions and possibly served you very well. Once upon a time some of those old strategies might have been life saving. However, you can choose to think differently now.

....

Collecting a thought cloud doesn't take long. The impact and influence of old thinking patterns from the past is very seductive. Notice we can no longer deny the power of these old thoughts. Notice how directly those thoughts connect to feelings and lead to behavior. Notice how often these clouds have instigated habitual responses. These thought clouds will continue to run outdated programs until the system gets an upgrade.

The whole pattern of your cloud is a work of art. It's a masterpiece to be viewed with great curiosity, compassion, and understanding. The dynamic may have served you well or held you back. Now you must decide to direct your thoughts more powerfully or they will continue to powerfully direct you. The choice is yours. Every miracle of healing begins with a change in thinking. This shift in consciousness requires a return to wholeness: remembering who you truly are.

Key points

▶ The collection of negative thoughts in your unconscious mind behaves like a virtual storm.

▶ Problems occur when thoughts set in motion long ago still govern what appears to be real today.

▶ When stress spirals collectively and joins together to build 'thought clouds' the combined effect is overpowering.

▶ A double bind is a conflict of choice between equally undesirable and opposing alternatives.

▶ Review the whole cloud from a higher perspective and it will never have the same power again.

▶ Once a cloud gets triggered, the end result is almost guaranteed.

▶ Thoughts will continue to run old outdated programs until you upgrade the system.

▶ Learn to direct your thoughts more powerfully or they will continue to powerfully direct you.

··

Choice Thoughts

My thoughts mirror my inner beliefs.

I cannot change what I do not know.

I can find my answers from within.

I interpret and understand my body's signals.

I celebrate my uniqueness and magnificence.

The thoughts I think right now can heal the future.

I am returning to wholeness, remembering who I am.

Chapter 7

Head in the Clouds

Everything originates from thought. Every creation, every invention, every work of art, every good or bad thing that happens, every decision has been preceded by thoughts originating in the past. These thoughts developed into complex thought clouds a long time ago; there they sit innocently and silently until some trigger switches them on.

The energy of the emotions generated by the thoughts maintains the cloud in operation mode. The greater the intensity of emotion, the greater the intensity of energy, and the greater the activity propelled by the cloud. Many thoughts appear to be quite neutral, objective, factual, or analytical on the surface. Yet on further exploration, you will discover that each thought moves in one of two directions. Imagine the 60,000 thoughts you think every day, all flowing as a stream of data. This flow of data moves toward the particular destiny according to the direction chosen by the type of thought.

Each thought represents one piece of data flowing in the stream. Emotion empowers the direction of that data. When you think positive, loving thoughts the data flows along with the current in your positive stream of destiny. Everything seems effortless; every move feels comfortable, harmonious, connected, and in sync with the universe. You feel a sense of inner knowingness. Luck and miracle-mindedness abound. You easily maneuver around any obstacles. The universe appears to support every decision you make and abundance flows.

The opposite happens whenever you think negative thoughts: comparing, criticizing, complaining, or focusing on lack. Then the flow of data turns in the opposite direction, going against the natural current. Sparks fly! The negative thoughts cause intense fear-based emotions, which result in system overload. Getting nowhere fast leads to frustration, anxiety, and more stress. Using more determination you have to work twice as hard just to hold your position. The situation becomes critical as you lose control, burn out with exhaustion, and the whole system crashes.

Notice the process can be reversed. You can turn around anytime you wish. When 'bad' things happen, it just means your thoughts were programmed to go in the wrong direction. Accept this as feedback instead of feeling punished. You have temporarily lost your way and therefore lost the protection that comes with being in the flow. Just turn around. Every moment offers you a new opportunity to choose different thoughts.

The metaphysical book *A Course in Miracles* says all thoughts opt for one of two choices: love or fear. There's no middle ground, no neutral, nor is there any truly objective viewpoint. Because our perception is influenced by thought clouds the reality we see will also reflect this polarity. To test this idea, take a piece of paper and draw a vertical line down the middle of it. At the top of one column write 'Love' and then 'Fear' in the other. Then examine each thought. Carefully assess whether the basis of each thought stems from love or fear or notice the direction it flows. Jot each thought down into the appropriate column. If it's unclear in which column to place a particular thought, consider all the other ideas associated with it, what purpose it serves, and for what reason it is important. For best results, ask a group of people to play the game and debate each one. For example the thought 'I want to heal this' sounds very positive and could be a statement for the 'Love' column when healing is perceived as a natural return to wholeness and acceptance. However it belongs to the 'Fear' column if healing is perceived as moving away from some undesirable dangerous malady. The direction of the thought depends not only on which words are used but also what those words mean. It is what's behind the thought that counts, not just the words.

After exploring how various thoughts connect within your cloud, it's simple to detect how, when, and where things went in the wrong direction. Let your feelings associated with each idea guide you. Negative feelings mean you have not chosen love. So how could those thoughts be turned around? How could you choose to think more lovingly? Some people use negative feelings like anger, frustration, or fear to motivate them, but the by-product of stress is counterproductive. For example, using anger to push yourself into working harder, being more competitive, proving a point, or getting revenge works in the short term, but the long-term cost will be a high degree of internal stress. Using anger in this way can become a habit that increases the stress in your body and also raises the stress levels of others in your environment.

Notice your thoughts, identify the feelings, recognize the decisions, and discover the origins. Be open and willing to make the choice to return to love. Change only takes as long as the time needed to overcome any inner resistance. Only your thoughts hold you back. However, sometimes the thought infrastructure requires several updates of correction before a better choice is made.

> '*You want to be happy. You want peace.*
> *You do not have them now, because*
> *your mind is totally undisciplined.*'
> A Course in Miracles, Anon

Change the channel

Choosing to think differently requires using your brain differently. Changing the channel in your brain makes it easier to make choices that heal. Did you know that the way you see acts as a switch? There are two ways to see through your eyes: focal vision and peripheral vision. Everyday focal vision means looking directly at one object at a time while scanning a scene. What happens outside of the chosen focus of attention gets ignored. The brain collects these snapshots and then builds its own virtual reality about your current environment.

Unfortunately because more than two million bits of information bombard the senses every second, the brain must delete a great deal of input to avoid going into overload. The conscious mind can't take in more than 10 bits per second. That means a massive deletion is occurring right now! In order to make sense of the incomplete input, the brain compares the bits you see to previous experiences. Then any missing bits get filled in from previously stored memories that match your accepted beliefs. So the brain reconstructs images rather than assessing new information. Just look around the room. You won't see any missing bits. Yet each eye has a blind spot created by entry of the optic nerve, so there's actually a patch on your retina where there are no rods or cones. Each eye has an area that cannot see at all. However the brain cleverly fills it in wherever you look. This means two things: no one really sees the whole of reality; and the limited version of what you do see gets distorted by the clouds of thoughts already in storage.

A simple shift to 'peripheral vision' has a profound effect. Using peripheral vision requires paying attention to what you see at the extreme edges of your visual field without moving your eyes away from your chosen focus. You can still see directly in front of you, but notice how the view becomes much wider, and you take in more of the whole scene. Why is this important? Even though the senses still can't process all two million bits of information per second, awareness does increase, the eyes do see the bigger picture and the brain therefore makes different connections.

....

EXERCISE
A different perspective with peripheral vision

Try this for yourself. Just choose a spot to focus on directly in front of you and don't allow your eyes to move. Then raise your hands up to the sides and wiggle your fingers where you can see them. Without shifting your eyes, slowly move your hands backward until you can barely see the fingers wiggle. Notice what happens. As you become more aware of the peripheral field, do other senses also become more acute? Do you see different things in the room and hear more sounds?

Practice peripheral vision throughout the day until you can switch your eyesight easily without having to wiggle your fingers. Using peripheral vision is the optimum learning state because it allows your brain to take in more information. Because there is less intense focus, there is less likelihood of triggering an old thought cloud. So peripheral vision also helps you stay calm, cool, and collected; it is the optimum for state management. People who practice martial arts use this kind of vision. As you turn your attention to dealing with individual aspects of your cloud, use peripheral vision to help you stay detached.

....

'We are what we think. All that we are arises with our thoughts. With our thoughts, we make our world.'

Buddha

Thought clouds: a virtual reality

The thoughts in your cloud represent a virtual reality created from past misperceptions, misunderstandings, deletions, distortions, generalizations, lack of information, and ignorance. Some thoughts may hook you into believing they are true facts, things that really happened. But how can you know what was truth and what was illusion? How can you be sure that your perception of past events was real? Different witnesses of an event rarely describe the same scene nor do they agree on the facts. Just try getting everyone in your family to agree on what happened during a particular family gathering in the past! Everyone notices different things, paints a different picture, and makes different meanings from the memories.

Can events of the future be known with any certainty? Just like everyone has their version of past events, they also have their predictions of the future. But this future can only be imagined and constructed by using memories of what happened in the past. The information in those memories may have been more fantasy than reality. So neither the future nor the past can be proved beyond all doubt. There are always different perspectives, interpretations, and possibilities. Truth can only exist in the present moment. However, even that is subject to distortion. What do you trust is true here and now? What criteria support that truth? What do you believe as evidence? What other truths could also be possible? Would everyone agree on the present? Notice there's an opportunity to choose what is true for you in the present, past, and future.

....

EXERCISE
Speak in the present

Try this little game with a friend. Commit to speaking only in the present tense. You gain a point for every statement in the present and lose a point for every statement referring to the past or future. Say absolutely nothing that is about the past and make no predictions about what might happen in the future. The past is defined as anything that happened a split second before, the future a split second after now. So, for example, if you are eating an ice cream and say 'this tastes good' then this is a past statement and loses a point. The time it takes for your brain to evaluate the taste makes it a statement about the past, especially as it also had to take time to evaluate whether or not it tasted good. The split-second delay of brain processing between experience and the expression means it is almost impossible to speak in the present. Similarly, if you glance out the window and say 'it looks like it will rain,' you are predicting the future based on comparisons with past memories.

One of the problems of communication is that it keeps us stuck talking about versions of the past that are subject to error and misinterpretation. As long as everyone is in agreement with what happened in the past, no one notices. But as soon as someone challenges this agreed version of reality, problems occur.

Have you ever experienced the virtual reality rides at Disneyworld? Even though you know the make-believe environment is safe, it doesn't take long before you feel genuinely scared! During computer simulations used for training pilots and astronauts, the mind and body adapt in no time at all, responding to the virtual reality as if it were real life. Heart rate and blood pressure immediately increase as the adrenal stress loop swings into action. Trying to make sense of things, the brain reacts to the new input incredibly quickly. The brain forgets that it's dealing with a fantasy. It doesn't take long before you begin to identify yourself differently within this virtual reality. You may start behaving differently and interacting with others as if you are this character in this virtual world. In a similar way, depending which thought cloud gets switched on or off, you think, feel, and act so differently it is almost like having another identity. This could be why people sometimes say 'I wasn't myself when I said that.' They have entered the virtual world of their past.

> *'If you believe that dreams can come true, be prepared for the occasional nightmare too.'*
> French proverb

The collection of thoughts in your cloud exerts a magnetic force that can pull you into its vortex so it is vital to know how to extract yourself. The two simple tools already mentioned help a great deal: deep breathing (see page 73) and peripheral vision (see page 139). Interrupting the pattern is another way to force your brain to shift gear. The faster you can break state and disengage from a thought cloud the better. The more intense the cloud, the more powerful the interruption needs to be. Anything that immediately changes your focus works well to shift your attention away from an undesirable thought cloud.

....

EXERCISE
Seven ways to interrupt a thought cloud

1. Move your body to disengage your brain
Changing your physiology exerts the most powerful shift of attention. Look up, get up, move about, go for a walk, laugh, sing, chant, drum, exercise vigorously, do yoga, dance, do anything that positively engages lots of body movement and deep breathing. When a cloud has been

triggered, stress hormones accumulate in the body very quickly. Movement helps to cleanse the excess adrenalin out of your body tissues and releases the tension.

2. Stop all thoughts

Internally shout 'Stop' or use a favorite mantra that works to drown out the trigger. Stop trying to figure out why things are the way they are, why people behaved the way they did, or what is wrong with you. Stop analyzing, stop excusing, stop rationalizing, and stop searching for reasons and explanations. These thoughts only perpetuate your negative participation in the cloud. Just notice the signals, signs, and clues that something has taken you out of alignment. Do your best to change the channel and focus your attention on something constructive.

3. Stop trying to fix it

Stop fighting the problem, resisting the reality, being in denial, or using massive willpower to turn it around, change it, control it, or make something happen. Stop being afraid that you are running out of time. The idea of doing battle, even fighting for life against a serious illness, becomes counterproductive when it increases stress. Relax and accept what is happening right now. Take one moment at a time. Let go and trust things always work out for the best. Keep directing your thoughts in the most positive direction you can. Keep imagining how good it will be when everything is fine again, as if it has already happened.

4. Stop blaming other people or outside forces

Stop all thoughts of being 'a helpless victim.' Stop running negative movies inside your head. Stop going over and over the same events. Stop attacking your body as if it were separate from you. Step back, switch gear, apply willpower and force yourself to think of something – anything – more positive. Remember you are much more than just a physical body. Reaffirm your desired future picture. Turn it over to a higher power. Ask for help.

5. Remember you can only be responsible for you

Your power equals your ability to choose how you respond to what is going on. When you return to your center, when you align with your true inner self, you will feel better, even if nothing else changes. Be specific and write down clear statements of how you feel (e.g. 'I don't like the way he/she talks to me' or 'Nothing is working out'). Add these to your thought cloud. Then let go and ask yourself how you would respond if you were already healed and feeling good. How would your true self respond?

6. Assume whatever has happened has a purpose

Even if only to test you or teach you how to stay more centered. Observe how it feels right now, with the intention of turning your thoughts in a positive direction. Put this into a wider context. Look at any negative statements you have written down, and expand your vision to notice the exceptions and positive elements:

◊ **Places:** *Where does this <u>not</u> occur, or where is it <u>not</u> true?*

◊ **Times:** *When is everything okay, or when does this work?*

◊ **Intention:** *What positive intention does each person have?*

7. Consider the alternative possibilities

Soften your gaze and consider all the possible alternative thoughts that could be applied to this: what could be good about this happening? How does it help you? What have you learned? What are exceptions or positive aspects of this? What can you appreciate differently now? What do you feel grateful for? What could be more important than this? What are you more willing to commit to? What is funny about this that you never noticed before? What will you think when you look back in 10 years' time? If your answers lead to positive feelings, you are on the right track. Discard the rest.

Whenever a desired goal doesn't materialize, the motivation to achieve that goal receives an extra boost of energy. Channel this extra energy into making sure your next attempt is more refined. Redirect your energy back into the flow, and reaffirm all the reasons why you want your goal. What will it get for you, what will it allow you to do or be? Once your goal is fully aligned with your purpose, put your trust in finding flexible ways of zigzagging back toward that true destination. Be determined. Decide you will do whatever it takes to get there.

'You cannot prevent the birds of sorrow from flying over your head, but you can prevent them from building nests in your hair.'
Chinese proverb

How to dismantle a thought cloud

The architecture of your cloud has taken up space in your mind for some time. Therefore these thoughts may seem so familiar that you never questioned their validity before. To avoid the risk of getting embroiled in the cloud, please continue practicing some of the ways to interrupt the pattern or work with a good coach or guide. It also helps to reconnect with your Higher Mind or an inspiring mentor who can look at the dynamics of the cloud with objectivity and wisdom.

Every cloud of thoughts is unique and therefore requires a unique set of solutions. You may discover more than one cloud, or find clouds that link with one another. Perfectly depicting your cloud is less important than challenging the key components. Look for the hot spots (see page 129), places where the energy seems to get particularly stuck in never-ending loops. If you intuit the most important area to tackle first, it saves time. However there is benefit in dismantling every thought so that the cloud completely dissipates and never returns. You may find some of the following key components in your cloud.

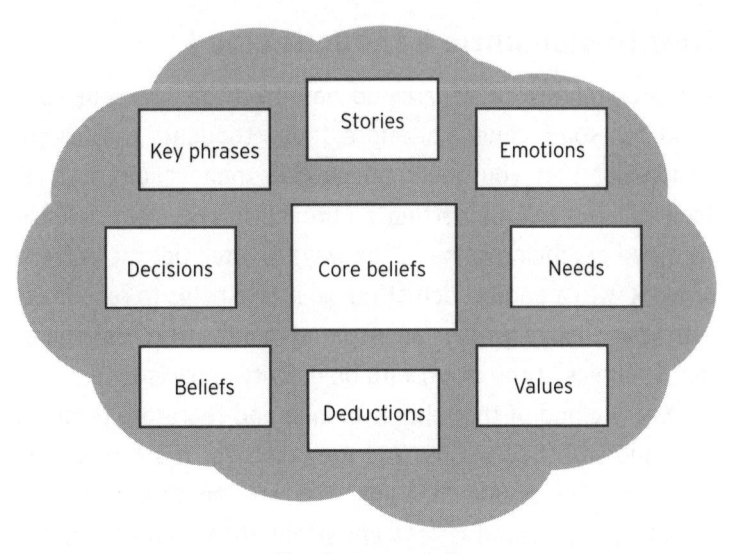

Cloud components

Overview of cloud components

▶ **Stories:** What important factors helped to originate this cloud?

▶ **Key phrases, decisions:** What is assumed as logical fact?

▶ **Beliefs, deductions:** What ideas and beliefs have been accepted as true?

▶ **Core beliefs:** What identity statements are being made?

▶ **Values and needs:** What is considered to be most important?

▶ **Emotions:** What specific emotions are being expressed?

At first the story connected to a particular problem might not be obvious. Use any related physical symptoms to point the way toward specific areas to question and explore. For example: my brain tumor affected only one hormone that happened to be crucial for fertility, pregnancy, and producing breast milk. Therefore my issues were probably related to having children, nurturing, and relationships. So the focus turned to finding stories in the past related to those topics. Any story that still holds pain, emotion, or lack of resolution will be most important. Either write down the story or have someone listen and collect the key elements and phrases.

> '*I just want to thank everyone*
> *who made this day necessary.*'
> Yogi Berra

....

EXERCISE
Key phrases, decisions – what is assumed to be true?

Pay particular attention to phrases that get repeated.
Statements that sound like facts are well worth capturing
because they usually disguise underlying less-conscious
beliefs. For this reason it can be extremely helpful to
write down each of the key phrases used to describe a
particular problem state and think about them later.
Then look at each phrase and ask: 'What else must be
assumed or presupposed as true in order to say such a
thing?' Uncover the hidden beliefs and check to see if
these make sense.

Decisions and deductions usually imply some action or inaction is involved. Sometimes the deduction is revealed by the relationship of one idea with another component in the cloud. This occurred so this must happen. Perhaps the logic no longer makes sense. Unfortunately, after such a decision was made, the alternatives got excluded from being considered any further. This lack of flexibility produces a certain kind of stuck state.

Here are some examples of what might be presupposed to be true in the following typical statements:

I'm only okay if I win.

Assumptions: I am not okay. I should be okay. Regard is conditional. Someone's judging my okay-ness. There's only one way to be okay: winning. The possibility of winning exists and therefore losing is also possible. Losing is not okay. I must be capable of winning. Therefore I feel pressured and driven to win. But if I do win and become judged as okay, it only proves the conditional clause. It doesn't prove my innate okay-ness. So it's impossible for me to feel okay whether I win or lose.

I'm trapped and must get out, but I can't – can't – can't!

Assumptions: Something holds me against my will. I am a helpless, powerless victim, lacking control over my state. There's nothing I can do to get out of this. There exists some kind of trap that I need to get out of now. Somewhere there's a place that exists outside of the trap, as well as a way to get there. I have repeated the same thoughts and the same actions to reach this place and consequently discovered the same inability and the same results.

I don't deserve attention, care, respect, love, justice, or healing.

Assumptions: Unlike others, I have been singled out as undeserving. Therefore I must be special and unique. I have to do something extra in order to deserve. Positive regard is conditional and can be bestowed or withheld by others. Whoever could bestow such qualities must also stand in judgment. The lack of attention, etc. proves that I'm a sorry victim of this negative judgment. I'm being punished.

I'm so awful no one could ever love me.

Assumptions: I'm different, special, and more awful than others who can be loved. I have won the competition! Awful is an undesirable state, judged by either me or by others or both. There are degrees of awfulness. To love me means totally accepting me, but this would require loving my incredibly high degree of awfulness. No one is capable of this (not even me), so no one is adequate in their loving. The defect is infinite.

I'm not good enough so I hide behind strong people.

Assumptions: The evaluation of what constitutes good is universal and agreed. There's a degree of good that is enough. Someone judges what is good and what is enough. The evaluation must be based on some comparison. Not good enough implies some level of being bad. It's possible and serves some purpose to hide behind others. I might not be good enough at hiding. Other people have some kind of strength that I don't have, but I'm clever enough to use them as shields.

If I fail I let people down.

Assumptions: *If it's possible to fail, it must also be possible to succeed. If I haven't yet failed, I must be succeeding at something. People will notice whether I fail or not. It's possible to know how others feel. If I fail people have no other option than to feel let down. I have conviction about people feeling let down. I am responsible for how people feel. I can control how others feel.*

People have betrayed me so I can't trust anyone anymore.

Assumptions: *There are universal definitions of betrayal and trust agreed by all people. People have done something that could be perceived as betrayal. I feel like the victim. If these people have made a mistake, then everyone else will always do the same. Therefore I distrust everyone. There was a time when I did trust. I know what trust is. If I can't trust anyone, then that must apply to me too. So I distrust myself.*

By simply stating what must be presupposed as true, you break the thought down into its component parts. Each key phrase rests on dubious facts, so this process is like shining a light in between the words to expose the erroneous rationale. The logic and assumptions don't stand up to scrutiny. When you break down your decisions and deductions into the assumptions they depend on, be sure to challenge each idea thoroughly. If any of the components make sense or seem true, ask your Higher Mind, your Heart, or a wise objective guide for help. Once you expose these false assumptions, it should be easier to let go of the stated belief.

'When we remember we are all mad, the mysteries disappear and life stands explained.'
Mark Twain

Each component is a small piece of data that may once have served some useful purpose, but now has become a barrier to your inner peace. The next step will be to find ways to reframe such a barrier, going around it, over it, under it, or possibly finding the doorway to walk right through it. Perhaps you already know some skills and techniques that work to challenge, reframe, or heal these old ideas. Proving the old thoughts to be invalid will help evaporate the cloud and blow it all away.

ACID TEST QUESTION
How will I know if the key phrases identified are the ones that need to be addressed?

First you should get a sense of recognition: you've heard these before. Despite the lack of logic, they should intuitively feel familiar. Identifying the assumptions should start opening up your thinking and your willingness to view things from another perspective. Challenging the reality and rationality of each component helps to loosen the energy behind the ideas. In the next chapter you will find more tools for undoing some of the deeper stuck beliefs.

Even if you feel stuck in a particular situation or you tell stories about how nothing ever changes in your life, every day is different. Embracing change, accepting it and not resisting it, is the key to increasing resilience. Life will trigger you to see how well you pass the tests and weather these changes. The only certainty about the world is that things will continue to change.

Remember, you may change your thoughts, your feelings or your sense of who you are, but your innermost center remains still. It's the eye of the hurricane, it's the sunshine after the rain, and it's the place where peace is power. Nothing ever stays the same. Change is the nature of the universe. Resilience requires the ability to live and move from your center like a martial arts warrior. The peace inside can reign even amidst chaos. No one knows what lies around the next corner. Anything can happen. Anything is possible.

Key points

▶ Peripheral vision helps you stay calm, cool, and collected; the optimum for learning and state management.

▶ The thoughts in your cloud represent a virtual reality created from distorted past misperceptions.

▶ Depending which thought cloud gets switched on or off, you think, feel, and act so differently, it is almost like having another identity.

▶ Thoughts exert a magnetic force that can pull you into the vortex of your cloud, so it is vital to know how to extract yourself.

▶ Perfectly depicting your cloud is not as important as challenging the key components.

▶ Cloud components can be stories, key phrases, decisions, beliefs, core beliefs, values and needs, emotions.

- Challenging the rationality of each component loosens the energy behind the ideas.
- Embracing change, accepting it, and not resisting is the key to increasing resilience.

....

Choice Thoughts

The quality of my thoughts produces the quality of my life.

Truth can only exist in the present moment.

I have many choices about how to respond.

I assume whatever happens will lead to something good.

I embrace change and accept it without resistance.

My thoughts may change but my inner center remains still.

Resilience means living and moving from my center.

Chapter 8

Cloudy with a Chance of Scattered Miracles

Most of us barely notice the 60,000 thoughts passing through the mind each day. We don't consciously pay attention to more than 10 percent of them. We don't consciously pick up the silent messages surrounding spoken words, voice tones, gestures, and behaviors. This lack of awareness leads to an erroneous belief that unexpressed thoughts and emotions are private. However many of these hidden thoughts unconsciously leak into communication.

In truth our brains are like sensitively tuned radio transmitters. During normal communication we receive not only the words, but also the energy, feelings, voice tone, body language, and subtle meanings. Words are not heard literally. Unconsciously, we do pick up what is unsaid. But hearing the unspoken thought sometimes causes confusion, mixed messages or misinterpretation. Most people remain totally unaware that their unconscious thoughts slip into the spaces

....

between the words. So when their unspoken feelings leak into the communication, they're unlikely to admit to them.

The energy of ideas, thoughts, beliefs, and emotions floating in your cloud creates a fog around communication. Despite using the most carefully chosen words, the message you send out reveals much more than you think or say with words. Listeners tune in to different frequencies and therefore receive your message on different levels. It's a bit like the curious phenomenon that Rupert Sheldrake talks about in his book *The Sense of Being Stared At*. He describes the uncanny sensory awareness of picking up people's silent thoughts and focus of attention.[1] Maybe you've had that experience: a sense of being stared at by someone standing behind you. Or perhaps you have had a thought about a long-lost friend. Then the phone rings and it's that same friend calling you! The unconscious mind tunes into other wavelengths of thought.

> *'You are not only responsible for what you say, but also for what you do not say.'*
> Martin Luther

Could it be that emotional states radiate energy in a similar way to the particles of an atom? Scientists used to puzzle over the fact that particles communicate with each other at a speed faster than the speed of light. Apparently each particle exists in many states at once, and each one is inextricably linked to others through a process called 'entanglement.' As one particle spins in one direction so a mirror particle spins in the opposite direction, no matter how far away. Einstein called this entanglement 'spooky action at a distance.'[2] Now this has become a widely accepted theory. It means that particles inside every bit of matter can instantaneously communicate through this form of mirroring.

Is it possible the energy of our thoughts and emotions can communicate in a similar way? Studies have shown that the closer the relationship and the more attuned we become to each other, the more we pick up those unconscious messages – even from the other side of the world. Perhaps when we direct loving thoughts toward others we cause vibrations in the particles that are entangled and resonating with ours. Maybe that's why close friends pick up the phone and call.

The Institute of Noetic Science performed a fascinating experiment with cancer patients. The close partner of the cancer patient was trained to beam compassionate intentions. After eight weeks of practice the two people were seated in different electromagnetically shielded rooms, with no possible way of communicating with each other. While the cancer patient was monitored on closed-circuit television, their loved one was asked to send compassionate intentions to their partner at random intervals. The measurements of response showed significant correlation of the physiological activity between the two unaccounted for by any conventional means of communication.[3]

There is no such thing as a private thought

While your thoughts and emotions transmit to others, your body cells are listening and resonating too. The atoms inside the molecules of every cell must be linked to each other through entanglement. These tiny charged particles are made of nothing but energy, whirling in the field of probability. According to quantum physics, what's experienced as reality turns out to be an infinitely changing fluid energy process.[4] The field of probability that gives birth to these energy particles is immediately affected by the energy of your thoughts. The 'Field' resonates according to your thinking. Fully appreciating how your thoughts create reality will raise your awareness of the immense power that you wield. Whether you choose to direct this power or not, your thoughts will continue to influence the Field.[5]

> '*All thoughts have power.*
> *They cannot be without effect.*'
> *A Course in Miracles*, Anon

Deep within a cloud you will usually find core beliefs radiating key negative thoughts that underpin all the other thoughts. You might hear them in the key phrases, intuit them from other beliefs, or distil them from the cloud as a whole. These negative identity statements are usually easy to spot. People believe them to be true so feel embarrassed and try to hide these core beliefs. Unfortunately, despite attempts to compensate for them by doing cover-up behaviors, other people pick up the negative self-concepts. Each person has their unique and individual core beliefs, but most of them come from variations of the following short list. There are many different versions. Do you have a favorite one?

EXERCISE
Core negative beliefs

For each different realm of life: work, love, family, sport, creativity, or health, think about which one might be present and give it a score on a scale 0–10 according to intensity.

Statement	Work	Love	Family	Sport	Creativity	Health
I'm not good enough... I'm inadequate...						
I'm not wanted... I'm unlovable...						
I'm not deserving... I'm unworthy...						
I'm not strong and capable... I'm weak...						
I'm not smart and clever... I'm stupid...						
I'm not perfect... I'm flawed, wrong...						
I'm not free... I'm a trapped victim...						

Take a moment to reflect on any negative 'I am' statements you commonly make in your thoughts, if not in your words. Notice if any of these appear in your cloud. Also take note that you could only hold such an idea if you also value the opposite. So 'I'm not good enough' means you must value being good. If you value 'being good,' notice part of you must know the difference between good and bad. Honor the part that desires to be good. Tune in to the part of you that really is a good person. Avoid dwelling on any of the negative identity statements. Focus on the implied positive meaning instead.

Oddly enough you would probably never say these negative statements to someone else: 'You are not good enough,' 'You are defective,' 'You are stupid,' etc. The direct attack would be too obvious. Yet core beliefs seem convincing maybe because they're so full of self-attack. They almost sound humble. They encourage staying small, being less than others, self-effacing and ultimately, having low self-value. This provides a clue as to their origin. Core beliefs often began in early childhood, sometimes at birth. Babies who are not welcomed into the world with love notice the negative energy that greets them. The brain senses the energy of the unfriendly environment and adds erroneous interpretations and reasons. Because very young children may not have words to describe their feelings, nor the wisdom to understand events, their unconscious minds make deductions full of errors.

Turning around strongly held beliefs or core beliefs isn't as simple as saying 'Don't be so silly, of course you're good enough.' Although affirmations work well for other beliefs, repeating something such as 'I am good enough, I am perfect, I love and accept myself' may not have enough power to reverse a deep-seated core belief. Some people who tried using positive affirmations reported the negative belief intensified because the brain knew the affirmation was a lie. Rationally trying to analyze the poor logic of a core belief may not do the trick either. These core beliefs sit deep within the unconscious mind, where rational conscious approaches can't reach them.

'My words fly up, my thoughts remain below:
Words without thoughts never to heaven go.'
William Shakespeare, *Hamlet*

Revisiting the origin of a belief

Revisiting the memory of the original event of the core belief helps. Just set the intention to discover what you need to know, then allow your Higher Mind to guide you back in time to when the belief first appeared. Reassess what happened in this early event, what was going on and who was present at the time. What decisions were made and what did you decide it meant? Appreciate the good intentions behind the actions throughout the story, and then apply your wisdom to understand it fully from different perspectives. Ask your Higher Mind for spiritual insights and truth until each aspect feels healed.

Time has a very curious effect on memories and emotions. Simply imagining being able to visit different times before, during, and after a significant event changes the ability to feel the emotion associated with that event. By imagining you can travel in time before and after the event, you can interrupt the certainty of the thinking strategy. The memory can then be more easily questioned, challenged, and adjusted.

People fear that imagining an old trauma means reliving the terrible event and re-experiencing the same intense emotions that occurred at the time. There is something strange about that. Doesn't it seem odd to have a strong reaction to mere imagination, when nothing is actually happening in the present moment? Phobias are particularly good examples. It's just a thought cloud triggering an outdated response. It is possible to learn how to switch your memory on or off. By imagining you could time travel back to before the event ever happened, or far into the future when everything is fine, the power of the old habit is weakened and you can switch off the response.

....

EXERCISE
Time travel

Try this yourself: think of a significant event that has happened recently. Answer the following questions and notice how it changes the way you think and feel.

◊　*Fully imagine being in the future, looking back at this event five years from now. How important does it feel?*

◊　*How much does this matter 10 years from now? Or 25 years from now? After it's fully resolved and in the past, how does it feel?*

◊　*Looking back from 99 years old, how different does it look as you review all the important events during your entire life?*

◊　*On the day after your funeral, reviewing the growth and evolution of your soul's journey, how would you describe this event?*

◊　*Imagine you could go back to being a very young child again, looking forward to your life with great anticipation. How does this child look forward to what will happen all through life?*

By fully experiencing what it feels like at these different times, the brain gets a compelling message about the continuous nature of life. Instead of overly focusing on one memory and allowing that to be all-important, we need to remember that life is full of other moments, other choices, and other possibilities. The perspective of time has a unique power. We view things very differently during each phase of life.

'Unknown magic is believing in yourself. If you can do that, you can make anything happen.'

Johann Wolfgang von Goethe

Negative core beliefs violate your true identity and sense of self-worth. They hold so much conviction, and it helps to loosen their grip by challenging, questioning, and reframing the thoughts that build them. This will also make sure the old thought structure never reinstates itself. Reframing means looking at things from different perspectives in order to provide a different meaning or find a different context where the same idea could be beneficial. The following questions, adapted from NLP, are designed to challenge what is believed to be real or true.

EXERCISE
Reality checks

Focus on only one belief, decision, or value at a time and write it down in one sentence, to stay focused. Ask each question and do your best to answer each one before moving on to the next. If you write down your answers, the weakness of old logic will become more apparent.

Reality strategy: What is your evidence?

◊ Is this true? Is this really true? What evidence verifies this?

◊ Is it true for everyone? Has it been true throughout time?

◊ How would you know if it weren't true?

Counter example: What are the exceptions?

◊ Was there ever a time when this didn't apply?

◊ Do you know people who have changed this?

◊ Will this be true every time? Forever?

Redefine it: What does this mean to you?

◊ What other meaning could this have?

◊ Who would you be without this belief?

◊ How do you treat yourself because of this?

Intention: What is the positive intent?

◊ Why do you think, or believe, or speak this way?

◊ What do you gain by this? What could you be trying to get?

◊ What could you be trying to prove or trying to avoid?

Higher values and beliefs: What's more important than this?

◊ What's more valuable than holding on to this?

◊ What other belief makes it possible to believe this?

◊ Is this belief aligned with who you want to be?

Outcome: What do you really want?

◊ What is a different outcome you could choose?

◊ What would your situation look like without this belief?

◊ What better belief would you like instead?

Perspective: What is your focus of attention?

◊ What small aspect of this is okay?

◊ What larger aspect of this could be beneficial?

◊ Where could this show up and not be a problem?

Consequences: What will inevitably occur if you don't change?

◊ What is bound to happen if you continue to think this way?

◊ What will never happen if you continue to think this way?

◊ Does that fit for you or do you see a reason to drop this belief?

Acceptance: What are you open and willing to accept?

◊ What can you honestly accept about this?

◊ How could this be perceived as integral to your experience?

◊ What does this give you and what can you do with that?

Surrender: What are you willing to let go of?

◊ Would you be willing to embrace this as it is? When?

◊   *Can you let go and give it permission to be the way it is?*

◊   *Could you look forward to the next time this happens?*

In order to answer these questions well, you will need to access your Higher Mind for alternative perspectives. This activity gets the brain to practice new neural pathways. The more you repeat the search for positive answers and convince yourself with updated information, improved perspectives, more intelligent arguments, and timeless wisdom the more you create new and better routes in the brain to take you to positive destinations. Each time you shift a thought, a mini miracle has occurred.

'Little drops of water wear down big stones.'
Russian proverb

Acceptance is the key. Practice embracing who you are right now: stop judging, blaming, and resisting. Your inner worth needs to shine out. Let go of prescribed plans, cultural expectations, and comparative evaluations. Accept your imperfections and the mistakes you may have made in the past. Maybe it's time to stop trying to be acceptable or normal. When you can look in the mirror and love and accept yourself exactly as you are right now, you will have more freedom to choose new thoughts and behaviors that align with your true values.

Values and needs

True values describe what is most important to us. What do we really value in life, in work, in relationships, and regarding health? What do we stand for? What footprint do we want to leave as our legacy? There will be a different set of values in each area. Sometimes these will clash with each other causing internal conflicts. Until we bring our values into awareness, they tend to remain unconscious. There's a tendency to take values for granted and assume that others hold the same values as we do. They don't! Values and needs are closely related but they are not exactly the same. Values have more to do with ethical principles: what is considered to be right or wrong, good or bad, as well as what's most important, useful, beautiful, desirable, healthy, etc. People will defend their important values and they will die to protect them.

Values explain why people do what they do. In his effort to understand what motivated criminals, psychologist Clare Graves developed an epistemology of human behavior based on the evolution of human needs. His theories are still incredibly insightful. As a child grows up, different values need to be met during each period. The way a child matures through different stages of development mirrors the way cultures have evolved through different existential levels over time. Values get determined by the needs people face in different circumstances. A baby values safety and security, a young child values adventure, a teenager values autonomy. People will violate some values in order to satisfy others, according to what is held as most important. A classic example would be someone who feels driven to make huge profits (valuing wealth) despite the cost of harming other values: health, relationships, or the ecosystem of the planet.

'What we call happiness in the strictest sense comes from the (preferably sudden) satisfaction of needs which have been dammed up to a high degree.'
Sigmund Freud

As long as you have a body, you will have needs. Human beings cannot live without air, water, food, warmth, rest, light, movement, and loving touch. You cannot live without these objective physical needs. However there are many less essential needs that are more subjective. Some needs support larger values. For example because you 'value' life, you 'need' air, water, and food. Sometimes the same word is used: you may 'value' honesty as a principle, and have a 'need' for honesty in daily interactions. You 'value' personal safety so you 'need' a certain amount of personal space as well as culturally acceptable demonstrations of respect. A perceived violation of a need or value has maximum impact. Powerful triggers always involve needs and values not being met. This may explain overreactions, such as when someone stands too close, stares too long, uses a loud voice tone, or waves their arms in gestures that don't match expected norms. It threatens the personal value of safety and the need for territorial space and respect.

The values that show up in your cloud might be polluted by outmoded ideas: what you used to think was important a long time ago. Look for statements that express evaluations, judgments, certainty, or ideas that used to be important. You can use the 'Reality Checks' exercise (see page 165) to question them. Then discover what you want to believe and value now. Values change and evolve with each stage of life. If you haven't reviewed your values recently, use the following exercise to clarify what is most important to you now with a specific area in mind: work, relationships, health, etc.

EXERCISE
What do you consider most important now?

◊   What top 10 values are important to you now?
(List them.)

◊   Do your actions, words, and thoughts support
those values?

◊   Are any of your values in conflict with each other?

◊   Are you willing to stand for and defend these values?

◊   Do your values fit with who you want to become?

◊   Are you 100 percent committed to living by
your values?

Where you spend most of your time, energy, and money
reveals what you really value. Even the things you
feel you have to do, such as hold down a job, pay the
mortgage, take care of the children, hold inherent values
that you have chosen to honor. Sometimes you may
notice a difference between what you think you value
and what actually receives your full attention. What you
think about most, what you talk about, and what you
feel inspired by all reveal aspects of your values. It can be
easy to think that life dictates what you have to do, but
everything you do is a result of the choices you have made
according to your values. By appreciating the personal
importance of these activities you can transform them
from being onerous duties into desirable choices.

It is healthy to reassess what really is important to you
on a regular basis. You may need to adjust your values as
you evolve or change your activities to match your values

in new ways. When something feels important enough, you will find a way to do it. Motivation depends on what you value, not on time, money, or knowledge. Maybe there's no right time to do something. Maybe you will never know everything you need to know. Maybe you need to make decisions regardless of the risk involved. What's most important to you now?

When you're fully committed to your highest values, you do things for the right reasons. You find it easy to stay motivated and persevere even when the going gets tough. You can handle higher levels of stress and feel more resilient. You demonstrate your values in your words, your actions, and the way you get your needs met. You draw on memories that strengthen and support you, keeping you more emotionally balanced.

'Be careful when speaking. You create
the world around you with your words.'
Navajo saying

Emotional glue

Whether or not you get your needs met determines what kind of emotion you feel and consequently your level of stress. Emotion acts like glue sticking similar memories together. Like a chain of Christmas tree lights, they all light up at once, making it possible to recall all the happiest times, all the sad occasions, or all the angry events, etc. It only takes one trigger to suddenly switch on all the memories in a particular chain. Instead of dealing with just one event, a cataclysm of all previous events light up and start flashing. Whether the memories cluster together in a jumble or events follow a tidy chronological sequence, the consequence of feeling their combined emotion all at once can be overwhelming. Happy chains feel like falling in love, but when negative chains get triggered, it feels traumatic. These emotional chains cause things to get out of proportion.

After you resolve the issues, address the needs, and reassess the values in the key event it's easier to let go of the old negative emotions. The emotional glue evaporates and the chain of events gets re-filed as separate memories stored in your museum of history. You can still revisit old memories individually, but because they no longer gang up on you, the emotions don't get triggered.

The meanings and decisions revealed in a thought cloud are more important than whether or not the memories being accessed are real. The objective is to swiftly identify, resolve, and let go of whatever ideas led to negative feelings. There are no mistakes. Every decision, every path, every action, everything that ever happened must have evolved from a previous choice. Each experience is perfectly designed for learning new insights, developing new qualities, receiving wisdom, evolving as a spirit, and becoming enlightened.

Key points

▸ Hidden thoughts unconsciously leak into communication; the message you send reveals much more than you think it does.

▸ People not only receive your words but also the energy, feelings, and the subtle meanings of what has been said.

- The thoughts in your cloud get transmitted in and around your communication.

- The closer the relationship, the more people pick up on the other's state.

- Reframing means looking at things from different perspectives in order to find other meanings or other contexts to shift the energy.

- Values explain why people do what they do; they are a coping system to deal with the problems of existence being faced.

- When you are fully committed to your highest values, you do things for the right reasons.

- You demonstrate your values in your words, actions and the way you get your needs met.

Choice Thoughts

*Every moment offers a new opportunity
to choose different thoughts.*

This experience is perfectly designed for learning.

I can persevere even when the going gets tough.

*I am curious to discover how things can
work out for the best.*

My Higher Mind provides the best alternative perspectives.

I welcome new insights, answers, and understanding.

I am evolving as a spirit and becoming enlightened.

Chapter 9

Forgiving the Unforgivable

The two forces of order and chaos oppose each other throughout the universe. Life is a constant process of pulling order from chaos or vice versa. A body originates from a chaotic explosion of undifferentiated cell growth to form an orderly system of tissues containing 80 trillion cooperative cells. Inside every cell, inside every molecule, inside every atom all the way down to the quantum particles in each atom, order is being chosen from the chaos.

Every body cell receives the energy generated by our thoughts and emotions. As each thought strums different chords, our cells dance to the different melodies played by our emotions. This music resonates throughout the body. Like the chaos of an orchestra tuning up, the noise can be jarring and unpleasant, but after lots of practice the same orchestra can play a beautiful symphony. Depending on our moods our emotions can be jarring and unpleasant or the most beautiful song of inner joy. The next step is to learn how to conduct this inner orchestra and bring more order into the chaos.

Receiving bad news intensifies the contrast between order and chaos. Bad news clashes with the expectation that life should be healthy, good, happy, and successful. For example, receiving a serious diagnosis can feel like punishment or the worst thing that could have happened. Struggling with tests, treatments, discomfort, pain, fear, decisions and interruptions makes life feel extra challenging, overwhelming, and chaotic. So it's common to think that fighting the disease must be the way to restore order. Winning this battle becomes the measurement of happiness and success. But struggling, fighting, and battles all make lots of unhealthy noise. What helps healing is to find that place of inner harmony where our thoughts resonate with joy, peace, and love.

Emotion can be defined as energy in motion, a propelling force. Just like amoebas seeking food, emotions propel us toward what we like or away from what we want to avoid. Of course we feel positive and negative emotions about what we want and what we don't want. However, setting a positive healing intention can be a little tricky. We need to be careful to avoid implying that we will only be happy when we finally achieve health, success, abundance, or peace. Does happiness actually depend on achieving the goal or can we choose to be happy right now?

> '*I never get tired of the blue sky.*'
> Vincent van Gogh

Honoring your feelings and emotions

To undo the path of illness we need to trace the stress back to the mental chaos associated with the event at the origin of the problem. In the original event beliefs and decisions were made depending on whether or not your needs got met. Values were established about what was good or bad, right or wrong. Notice the link between the needs, values, and beliefs. These led to the feelings and emotions according to the needs that didn't get met. The negative feelings increased stress levels. Then the stress that got suppressed into the body started developing symptoms.

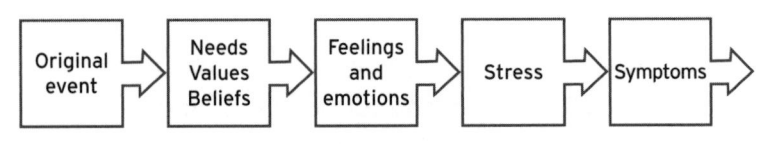

The symptom chain

A simple pathway to healing starts with addressing each part of the chain in reverse. First pay attention to the symptoms, metaphorically listening to the messages the body wants to communicate. Trace this back to what caused the stress, what feelings and emotions were involved. Then identify the needs that weren't met, the decisions that were made and the values and beliefs that formed. Finally search the past for the original event when this chain of thinking first began. Particular aspects of the original event may need to be re-examined with mature wisdom and then forgiven. Those earlier ideas were probably programmed into the mind, long before we learned how to reason or make wise decisions. If negative emotions rule our responses that means some event hasn't been fully digested and understood. Each emotion provides distinct clues about the type of experience that gave birth to them.

For example, all the words used to describe anger, including rage, irritation, and frustration, wave a red flag about something or someone violating your values. When someone trespasses on your territory, invades your space, breaks your rules, or threatens what you hold precious, anger naturally jumps in to defend you. Emotions respond quicker than thinking. Your feelings react instantly, long before your mind has time to correctly interpret what is going on in your environment. Be very grateful and pay attention when you feel strong feelings. Your emotions work on your behalf. They are not the enemy. How they get expressed is the problem.

> *'If you are patient in one moment of anger,*
> *you will escape a hundred days of sorrow.'*
> Chinese proverb

When emotions flare up, it helps to keep things in perspective. Whenever you catch negative emotions stirring up your thought clouds, stop and make sure you have interpreted the situation as correctly as possible. Here are some helpful questions to ask in order to keep a cool perspective.

....

EXERCISE
Keep a cool perspective

◊   *Could I have misinterpreted the situation?*

◊   *What if this was just an unintentional mistake?*

◊   *Have I looked at it from different perspectives?*

◊   *Do other people care for me despite this mistake?*

◊   *What positive intentions does each person have?*

◊   *Do other people actually know what is important to me?*

◊   *Have I ever made my standards clear to others?*

◊   *Do other people share those same values or rules?*

◊   *Am I sure those values or rules are the right rules?*

◊   *Would it be useful to re-evaluate what is really important?*

◊   *Could I be more flexible and let go of being in control?*

◊   *Does it have to be like what has happened in the past?*

Feelings of fear send clear signals about danger in your environment. Your survival might be at stake. All other variations of fear: anxiety, worry, nervous trepidation, inadequacy, panic, and terror want you to take immediate action to protect yourself. Check whether the threat is real or imagined. Perhaps some mental preparation is needed. What needs to be evaluated or avoided? Where can you get help or safety? What are you being called to do? If events feel beyond your control, make the decision to have faith. Ask for help and trust that no matter what happens, there will be a way through.

> *'Always do what you are afraid to do.'*
> Ralph Waldo Emerson

Sadness, disappointment, despair, depression, or other gloomy feelings let you know that some desired goal may never happen. Do you know what that expectation was? Maybe there has been a loss, maybe you have missed out on something forever, or maybe you could choose a new goal and not feel so hopeless. Guilt, shame, regret, humiliation, and embarrassment feel so hard to live with because they remind you that you have violated your values. You haven't lived up to your expectations. But do you dwell on those mistakes so often that they have accumulated into a mountain? The more you hold on to guilt, the bigger the mountain grows. It serves no one. A better idea might be to commit to never making the mistake again, learn from the experience and forgive yourself.

> *'There is no miracle you cannot have when you desire healing. But there is no miracle that can be given you unless you want it.'*
> *A Course in Miracles*, Anon

No situation is permanent. Everything depends on what perspective you take. Negative feelings knock you off center and trigger obsessive thought-cloud activity. Encourage your mind to focus in a more positive way. When you calm down it's easier to develop a more resilient attitude. In order to reinforce better brain pathways, here are some positive suggestions to put into practice. Ask yourself what would look different if you did the following?

....

EXERCISE
Positive choices

◊   *What if you got more rest and fresh air?*

◊   *What if you clarified exactly what you want?*

◊   *What if you were both motivated <u>and</u> patient?*

◊   *What if you chose how you want to feel about it?*

◊   *What if you focused first on the highest priorities?*

◊   *What if you could let go of all your expectations?*

◊   *What if you did not have to do everything now?*

◊   *What if you removed the pressure to succeed?*

◊   *What if you remembered you are good enough?*

◊   *What if you viewed this through eyes of love?*

How would it feel if you presupposed there must be some empowering meaning behind events? Could it be possible that what has happened is not a bad thing, you may not have lost anything, that it was a lucky escape? Could it be possible the loss signifies the closing of one door so that a new door can open, full of better opportunities?

Your emotions can direct your search to the precise early event that needs to be resolved. Typically most people want to focus on the most recent hot event that still bothers them. Although recent events may need resolution, it's much easier to do so after healing the origin in the earliest event. Surprisingly the origin usually means an event prior to the age of seven, especially if you don't remember your childhood. Remember, the programs unconsciously installed in your brain as a child become the brain structure that governs perception and causes repetitive problems later on. Working on more recent events may not reach the earlier part that needs to be resolved. Negative emotions also indicate that something needs to be forgiven.

Just thinking about what needs forgiveness may jog your memory to recall events with negative emotions still attached. What situations feel totally intolerable? Who or what do you judge, hate, condemn the most? What deserves punishment or justifies revenge and retaliation? What bad behaviors would you never ever do? Who would you least like to be like?

> *'Some cause happiness wherever they go;*
> *others, whenever they go.'*
> Oscar Wilde

We usually find it easy to identify who or what situation caused us most pain. What's more difficult is to genuinely want to forgive. Misunderstanding what forgiveness really means, some people stubbornly hold on to their reasons for judgment and condemnation. Thinking that forgivingness condones bad behaviour, excuses wrongs, and supports injustice are common mistakes. But forgiveness doesn't mean pretending it never happened, nor does it mean letting the perpetrator back into your life.

Forgiveness sets you free

The forgiveness you feel in your heart counts more than what you say. When you have fully forgiven, the past will no longer govern your future. You will be able to move on, be who you really came to be, and give your best. Your energy will no longer be drained owing to you holding on to the past. Your stress levels will reduce and your good health will increase. It doesn't make sense that you should suffer in order to uphold justice. It's not fair if your life feels angry and full of pain while perpetrators thrive and feel oblivious. Holding on to blame, judgment, or revenge doesn't work. It affects you, your health and your life, not those who were at fault.

> *'Forgiveness paints a picture of a world*
> *where suffering is over, loss becomes*
> *impossible and anger makes no sense.*
> *Attack is gone, and madness has an end.'*
>
> *A Course in Miracles*, Anon

The myths about forgiveness start with the fear that it will allow perpetrators off the hook. If guilty people get away with doing bad things then there is no justice for the wrongs committed. Believing wrongs must be remembered in order to honor the victim justifies thoughts of revenge. Some people refuse to forgive until the perpetrator acts contrite, shows remorse and begs to be forgiven. They think they need to understand why the wrong was committed before they can forgive. This rarely helps. Being the judge makes them feel important, powerful, morally superior, better than others. By blaming someone else, they get to feel more innocent themselves. They abhor looking weak, being vulnerable, or being pushed around. They prefer feeling righteous. People get addicted to the energy surge that anger gives them. They don't want to turn the other cheek, or be a doormat, or roll over and play nice. They say things like 'Forgive, but never forget,' which actually means never forgive.

Forgiveness doesn't have to take a long time, although it often does. However much or little you can forgive right now helps. Each layer of forgiveness is a step in the right direction. It's about forgiving the person, not the mistake that was made. Forgiveness is a choice you make for your sake. Forgiving helps you restore your sense of trust and love. It can be done whenever you feel ready.

'We are shaped by our thoughts; we become
what we think. When the mind is pure, joy
follows like a shadow that never leaves.'

Buddha

Signs that forgiveness may be needed

Negative emotions and traumatic events are obvious
invitations to forgive. Less obvious signs include being held
back in your life, being ill, or feeling stuck. Sometimes it's
about forgiving yourself, and other times it could be about
blaming someone in the past. What was never given, what
was withheld, what was taken away? If your life could be
completely wonderful and totally successful, who would be
vindicated? Who would get to think they did a good job? If you
have health problems, serious illness, lack of fitness, weight
problems, or addictions to drink, drugs, smoking, gambling,
sex, food, or caffeine ask who gets the blame for that? If you
generally don't take care of yourself or spend lots of energy
compensating or distracting yourself from feeling bad, what's
that about? Whose fault is it when your relationships suffer or
you feel unfulfilled, lack motivation or feel life is meaningless?
When you run out of people to judge, who or what else gets
the blame?

When you are ready to forgive, remember what counts is
what happens privately inside your heart. No words need to
be spoken. No one has to be let back into your life unless you
choose that. Forgiveness means acknowledging that a mistake
was made and then letting it go. It does not mean overlooking
it or pretending it didn't happen. Forgiveness is not about
saying nice words.

EXERCISE
20 Questions to help you forgive

1. What is more important to you than the mistake that was made?

2. Is it possible that life on Earth includes learning from mistakes?

3. Are you aware of the positive intentions behind those mistakes?

4. Is it likely that people make bad choices due to ignorance?

5. Can you imagine the innocent, ignorant child living inside whoever made those mistakes?

6. Is it possible to forgive the child and put aside the mistake?

7. Could you accept this had to happen as part of life's journey?

8. What would your Higher Mind say about honoring your values?

9. Could you make being loving more important than holding on to grudges?

10. How much can you let go and forgive today?

11. Because true vulnerability is invincible, can anything actually hurt you?

12. For your sake, will you do whatever it takes to heal this?

13. Will you take the next step and allow truth to show itself?

14. *Do you choose love and appreciate everyone, including yourself?*

15. *Would you be willing to give your love to those who need your help?*

16. *Could you put your trust in the Divine plan or your destiny?*

17. *Could you deserve to receive, and feel innocent and at peace?*

18. *Could you have faith, bless others, and the whole situation?*

19. *Could you ask for help, turn it over to God, and let go?*

20. *Do you realize that until those who should have known better really do know better, they'll just continue to make the same mistakes?*

When the fear of being attacked prevents full forgiveness, the spiritual concept of true vulnerability might help. True vulnerability rests on the principle that we are all part of the Divine spirit, magnificent, powerful, innocent, and full of universal love or God. Being part of God means our spirit is immortal and invincible. Therefore nothing can hurt this real part of who we are. The body can be attacked and hurt, but not the spirit. When we remember we are more than just our bodies, we can be fearless and totally vulnerable. In this way being vulnerable becomes the most powerful energy force in the universe and forgiveness is easy.

There may be groups of people you need to forgive. A very successful businessman had a problem controlling his angry temper. Because he worried about being a bad example for his young children, this motivated him to improve. His favorite book, *Think and Grow Rich* by Napoleon Hill, inspired him to work hard at containing his anger and curb his swearing. But to his dismay, this didn't work very well. Certain triggers still made him explode, especially when his stress levels got too high.

His pet peeve was what he called 'the age of no responsibility.' He felt incensed with anger when he read newspaper articles about famous people behaving badly who said they 'couldn't help what they did,' owing to bad childhood experiences. He believed people should be fully responsible for their behavior instead of hiding behind these limp excuses.

What he failed to notice was that he, too, was guilty of the same behavior. His anger pattern indicated some unconscious trigger probably stemming from a cloud of unresolved childhood experiences. Perceiving a problem in someone else's behavior usually indicates a projection of what lurks in your mind. Either you do the same thing or you do the mirror opposite. Both are flip sides of the same pattern. Some people claim they would never dream of behaving as badly as other people do. So they work extremely hard to appear very good. Or they treat their bodies badly and yell at themselves harshly.

The concept of reality as a projection resonated with this man's love of mind over matter. So he easily understood how he could only perceive faults in others if he also did similar things. It didn't take him long to discover that everything he criticized in others, he also did himself. In fact this helped him identify other issues that he most needed to heal. Not only did he become more compassionate about the mistakes other people made, but he also became less judgmental and more forgiving. The people who used to bother him so much now made him curious to find out what he needed to resolve in himself. His shift in thinking also made him a more tolerant father to his young children.

> *'To forgive is to heal.'*
> *A Course in Miracles*, Anon

If you have trouble forgiving yourself...

If you have regrets about something because you thought you knew better, remember that learning doesn't always reach all parts of the mind. Have you ever said to yourself, 'I should have known better'? You may have been exposed to learning moral principles, given lessons in proper behavior, and taught spiritual ideals. You may even talk about those ideals and believe they are true for you. But until these high ideals trickle through to your unconscious mind that updated programming hasn't been fully accepted. Part of you doesn't live by your words. Until you demonstrate those principles in how you behave, how you interact, what you think and do, you have not yet absorbed and integrated those ideas.

If a part of your mind still subscribes to an old set of values and beliefs, be forgiving. You need to access that part, discover why it holds on to outdated ideas. Until you fully correct the old mistake, different thoughts are impossible. The old ideas fill the brain and leave no space for new ways of thinking. Like a small child, this part of the brain needs your kind compassion, someone to help it gently grow up, understand and acquire wisdom. Just like a young child learning how to walk, this part of your mind may fall down a few times in the process. When you fully walk your talk, your words, your energy, and your actions will be congruent.

If you have trouble forgiving your body...

Sometimes it can feel like your body has let you down and sabotaged your best plans. If you detect some inner judgment, blame or anger toward some flaw, dysfunction, illness, or bodily affliction, you must have dissociated or separated yourself from your body. This mistake stems from not fully appreciating the difference between the conscious and unconscious mind. Of course you have not consciously created problems in your body. However your unconscious mind runs your body: your breathing, heartbeat, digestion, immune system, muscle movement, and even your emotions. If your body is like a computer printout of every thought, every memory, and every emotion you've felt over time then it is obvious that your body is innocent and deserves nothing but forgiveness. In fact as soon as you stop blaming and attacking your body, it has a much better chance of putting things right. Why not appreciate how hard it has always been working on your behalf? Accept what cannot be changed, let go of whatever hinders normal functioning and free up the healing process.

If you have trouble forgiving someone else...

If you have trouble forgiving someone else for what they did, you have a wonderful opportunity to discover some deeply hidden aspects of yourself. As previously discussed, your senses take in only a fraction of the total information available. Then the brain ignores and rejects information that doesn't match what is already in storage. So you perceive only what matches previously held beliefs, therefore your version of reality must reflect what's inside your mind. In this way, perception is projection, a mirror of the mind. What you see in others mirrors what's in your mind. That means the actions done by others must reflect some memory, thoughts or ideas in your mind. If you judge their actions then somewhere, somehow, you probably thought of doing the same yourself. It may look slightly different and may be directed toward yourself rather than others, but in essence it will be the same.

It can be difficult to recognize where you committed similar wrongs. Especially when the misdemeanor is extreme, such as betrayal, deception, violence, murder, or war. Yet looking deep within, have there been times when you may have betrayed your values, lied about having good intentions when you were actually trying to get what you wanted? Have you ever directed violent thoughts toward a part of your body when it let you down? Have you battled to get rid of some health problem, like waging a war against cancer? Until you discover your personal source of such troublesome thoughts, they continue to show up in your environment to get your attention.

Therefore, because the people you most condemn provide clear examples of what you never want to be like, in a way they become your teachers. Once you identify and eradicate the mistake they highlight for you, the opportunity to grow is yours. So you could almost feel grateful to them for playing the bad guy in your movie so you could learn this lesson.

> *'Always forgive your enemies.*
> *Nothing annoys them so much.'*
> Oscar Wilde

If you have trouble forgiving God...

If you have trouble forgiving God or wherever you put the blame for atrocities, you have an opportunity for enlightenment. In physics the law of conservation of energy states that the total amount of energy remains constant over time. Energy can neither be created nor destroyed, but only transformed from one state to another. The refusal to forgive God for bad things that happen holds a lot of energy. It also implies a belief that life should only be good, fair, just, and kind. Everyone should have perfect health, happy relationships, enough money, safe homes, and be singing hymns of joy and peace. How realistic is that? How boring would that be? Notice who gets to define what's good. Notice a very current timescale must be implied instead of God's eternity. When mistakes and bad things happen, it eventually leads to transformation, growth, learning, and enlightenment. Could that be the ultimate good purpose for those events? If God deserves to be dethroned for making a mess of things, notice who gets to do the job. Let go of any negative judgment and transform it into trust. Forgiveness will free your energy for a better purpose.

Remember the universe pulls order from chaos and vice versa; it's an ongoing process. Like yin and yang, the two forces complement each other. Accept both as essential parts of the journey. What can you accept about where you are right now, and what new options then open up? You can transform the worst events by searching for the benefits: past, present, and future. Imagine there could be a higher purpose for this experience. How could it be an important part of your evolution, your growth and mission in this life? Suppose you could learn something from this, and wonder what that might be. Believe something good will come of this, and it will.

ACID TEST QUESTION
How do you know if you have forgiven?

The first thing you notice is a feeling of peace. Your mind no longer wastes energy thinking about the offensive person or event. Instead of grumbling and processing in the background like a computer doing backup, your brain is free to focus on life again. You feel less stressed. You may even forget about the whole incident. When you do think about the person involved, there is a sense of compassion and understanding. Can you honestly wish them well and sincerely hope for their learning, growth, and evolution? When you genuinely feel okay about them being happy in their life, when there is no resentment if they prosper, you have fully forgiven.

Some people believe it is impossible to genuinely accept the unacceptable. What might you lose by being more accepting? What are the reasons to refuse? Continuing to hold something as unacceptable means more judgment, comparison, condemnation, and a lack of forgiveness. That uses up too much energy and brainpower. Who suffers as a consequence? The opposite must also be true. Acceptance sets you free, raises your energy, clears your thoughts, and makes you stronger and more resilient. Your new choice of thinking may demand a complete turnaround. The reality of your perceptions must be challenged. Instead of believing the limited input of what you see, hear, and feel; instead of merely accepting rational deductions and reasoning, you need to suspend such judgment and be willing to contemplate alternative possibilities and forgive.

'Better indeed is knowledge than mechanical practice. Better than knowledge is meditation. But better still is surrender of attachment to results, because there follows immediate peace.'
Bhagavad Gita

The thought-miracle shift

Reflecting on all the different aspects of your thought cloud, it may now be possible to acknowledge the positive benefits of the whole experience and appreciate the perfection of the path. As philosopher Friedrich Nietzsche said, 'Amor Fati' (love your fate), which is, in fact, your life. Notice what you have gained as a result. Note that different opportunities have opened up. Appreciate what you have learned. Celebrate the new qualities of character you have grown and developed. Even a small shift in perspective can be profound.

When I asked myself these questions about my long healing journey, it completely changed my perspective. Instead of viewing my tumor as my enemy, instead of focusing on how to get rid of it, instead of allowing my thought cloud to use up my brain energy, I began to appreciate all the benefits I had received along the way: people I had met, knowledge I had gained, life-changing experiences around the world, a new career, a more relaxed way of living. When I realized how the tumor had influenced the choices I made and helped me become a better version of me, I felt nothing but humble gratitude. In that instant it became my friend and guide. My stress evaporated, my thought cloud blew away.

Your personal resilience question

Would it be useful to have a shortcut to thinking this way? What if there were a question you could ask yourself in the heat of the moment? A profound idea can turn your thinking around. You can create such a question as a helpful reminder to follow good thoughts instead of falling into old habits. Design a question that works for you. Make sure it taps into ideas that will shift your thinking and bring in true wisdom. Here are a few samples to give you ideas:

▶ What can I do with what I have?

▶ How can I make the best of what is?

▶ Where is the good in this?

▶ What could be good about this?

▶ What good can come from this?

▶ What would love say, do, or think?

Make sure you keep a record of your personal resilience question and practice it often. Perhaps you could keep it as a reminder on your phone, or make a metaphorical representation in pictures, symbols, drawings, or music. The more you make use of your question, the more power and energy it will have to help you when you need it most.

The best energy for attracting any kind of success is gratitude and acceptance for what you have already received. This positive state of being acts like a magnet. After you have turned around the thoughts in your cloud, and after you let it all go, there is nothing to prevent your attraction energy from manifesting what you want. Have an attitude of trust and abundance follows. New possibilities open up and everything becomes available. Being true to yourself guides your choices and points you toward a brighter future.

Say 'Yes'

When you can say 'Yes' to life and 'Yes' to whatever happens, that means positively accepting what is. Acceptance allows you to make the best of things and move on, instead of staying stuck in the past. 'Yes' conveys receptivity, making you a magnet for good energy. Such creative responsiveness will transform any troubling situation. The antidote to holding on and being stuck is acceptance and being open to receive. Saying 'Yes' aligns with your higher purpose and willingness to be led by spirit.

Saying 'Yes' means you are choosing love and peace instead of fear and judgment. Choosing peace above all else activates the attitude of 'I can do this.' Saying 'Yes' means making the decision to commit, to persevere and to do whatever it takes, even if that means letting go of things along the way. The moment you genuinely say 'Yes' you return to inner truth and joy. Then it becomes easy to face any crisis, climb the towering mountain of any problem and walk the hero's path with total willingness, curiosity, and courage.

Key points

▶ To undo the path of illness you need to trace the stress back to the mental chaos associated with the original cause.

▶ Your feelings react instantly, long before your mind has time to correctly interpret what is going on.

- Presuppose there must be some empowering meaning behind every event.

- Until those who should have known better really do know better, they just continue to make the same mistakes.

- The brain ignores and rejects information that doesn't match what is already in storage.

- You know you have forgiven when you genuinely feel okay about everyone being happy in their lives.

- Even a small shift in perspective can be profound, so celebrate every new quality you develop.

- With an attitude of trust, abundance follows, new possibilities open up and everything becomes available.

Choice Thoughts

My thoughts can heal instead of causing stress.

Reality will shift as I make new choices and let go.

I am willing to take the next step and allow truth to show itself.

When I have fully forgiven, the past will no longer determine the future.

I accept that this had to happen as part of my journey in life.

I am asking for help, and turning it over to my Higher Mind.

True vulnerability is invincible, so nothing can really hurt me.

Chapter 10

Fly above the Clouds

Where I live in London thick clouds often cover the sky, making it dark and gray. So it never ceases to surprise me whenever I take off on a plane that as soon as it rises above the clouds, the sun is always shining brightly. Dazzled by the light, my eyes take a moment to adjust. The same gray clouds that seemed so heavy, dark, and gloomy from below, now look bright white and fluffy. The sky above is clear and blue. This quick change of perspective immediately lifts my heart. My mood becomes sunny and free.

The same is true of thought clouds. Change your perspective by rising above them. Then the sunshine of your Higher Mind makes everything look different. As you look down on the cloud below, the problems, issues, and thoughts dissipate into mere wisps of old memories. Immediately everything seems brighter and sunnier. New understanding, compassion, and a sense of peace put a smile back on your face. Of course when you feel good you smile, just as when you feel cross, you frown. However some interesting research suggests that the facial feedback loop works just as well in reverse. Simply by changing your expression, you can affect how you feel.

In 1872 Charles Darwin was one of the first people to notice that expressing emotions can influence the feelings. 'The free expression by outward signs of an emotion intensifies it,' he wrote. Psychologist William James took this idea further, postulating that if a person does not express an emotion, the emotion is not even felt. More recent research studies confirm Darwin's observation: expressing an emotion raises awareness of it and increases the feelings. Unexpressed emotions decrease awareness of the feelings; however, these emotional energies don't disappear. They sink into the body and show up in other ways: changing your mood or attitude.

Association and dissociation

Being able to step in or out of an emotional state is a particular skill that can be very useful. Generally speaking we like to associate into positive feelings and any physical experience that feels pleasant. Amplifying and expanding good feelings is as easy as paying more attention to everything we like about what is being seen, heard, felt, smelled, tasted, or thought about. By stepping into the moment, associating into your body, and increasing sensory awareness, your experience becomes more intense, particularly if you allow your face, voice, gestures, and movement to express how you feel. You'll feel more enthusiastic, more present, and the experience will be more vivid. Try being fully associated as you eat your favorite food. Your enjoyment will double and you'll need less of it to feel satisfied.

Dissociating from your feelings helps when you need to avoid pain. Whether the pain is physical or emotional, by dissociating from your sensations and taking your attention elsewhere, you can manage all kinds of difficult situations better. Just choose to focus your mind on something completely neutral or different. Be like Mr. Spock from *Star Trek* who had no ability to feel emotions. Keep your face impassive, your gestures and movements minimal and controlled. Imagine stepping out of your body, or being in the past or future where there's no problem. Disengage from what is going on. Use your 'resilience question' to direct your thoughts more positively. Trust there will be a way through whatever you are experiencing and imagine you have reached that desired future solution already. Dissociating allows you to think and act more rationally. Keeping your cool makes it easier to see more options and make better choices.

> *'One word frees us of all the weight*
> *and pain in life. That word is love.'*
> Sophocles

Stepping in and out of feelings

The way you describe a situation can help you switch between association and dissociation. Notice that in order to step into your feelings, you say 'I feel…' 'I say…' I think…' 'I want…' 'My feelings…' 'My needs…' 'My views…' 'My beliefs…' Use the pronouns 'I, my, me, mine' when you want to keep firmly in your shoes. Your words describe your experience. Expressing how you feel may show authenticity, or it may indicate a demand. When dealing with physical pain, there are times when it helps to go into the pain instead of resisting it. To feel it without fear allows your body to relax and calm down. Relaxing helps to relieve the pain.

At other times, it might be better to disengage from feelings. Dissociate from what is going on by speaking as if everything is separate from you: 'It, he, she, they, this, that, the body part, the pain, etc.' Then you become a disembodied observer, curious to watch events unfold. From this objective position it's possible to review, analyze, and dispassionately assess what's going on. Try shifting your internal dialogue to make observations using these third-person descriptions and you'll find it helps to reduce your emotional stress. Make your self-talk say what he or she did instead of what you did.

Sometimes not expressing your feelings helps keep things calm until more rational communication is possible. Sometimes dissociation is a form of avoidance. Sometimes it's a necessary escape from fear or a backlog of old unresolved feelings. When dealing with pain, it's possible to dissociate so well that painkillers become unnecessary. Hypnosis uses a form of dissociation that is so effective, surgical operations can be performed without anesthetics.

When my five-day headaches gave me intense pain, I used both association and dissociation effectively. When the pain was incredibly unbearable, I would 'hold' the part and imagine melting into it. By fully associating into the pain, I discovered it wasn't as bad as I feared. Instead of recoiling and resisting, I would feel, listen, smile, and explore every aspect of the sensation. To my surprise this immediately lessened the pain. As I became more curious to notice the sensation, color, radiation, heat, tingling, and any related emotions, I gradually became more attuned to what was going on in my body.

At other times I would choose to dissociate from the pain and pay attention to other parts of my body where it felt good. By focusing on the places where all was well, I could relax and even encourage the other parts of my body to remember how good they could feel. But when the pain was too intense, there were times I had to completely dissociate by imagining I could step outside of my body. Of course while doing this I would also rest, give my body support, and do anything I could to assist physical recovery.

When I had to function in my professional life, I used a different kind of dissociation by making a bargain with my body. Before I dissociated from the pain, I would remind my body how important it was for me to fulfill my purpose. Then I'd promise to take time off later and give my body my full attention. After making these promises, I'd negotiate: I'd ask my body to please reduce my symptoms long enough to allow me to do whatever I needed to do. Usually it would agree. Then later on, I'd fulfill my promise and associate back into my body to deal with whatever needed to be addressed. Pain in the body is an important signal, but it is often out of proportion to the actual problem, and often far away from the real source. Pain is often referred along the nerve pathway from the cause to a distant location. So as long as there is no danger of causing more harm, a temporary dissociation can allow you to be able to function.

Pain has a strong emotional component. Shifting the emotions from stressful to peaceful immediately reduces the sensation. About 50 percent of the brain's neurons serve the face and mouth; therefore the feedback loops from facial expressions create powerful neural pathways to and from the brain. Physically smiling stimulates the brain to release happy endorphin hormones. Surprisingly it doesn't matter whether the smile is real or fake. Any smile evokes the same mood-elevating response throughout the body. Fake smiles held long enough have a very real effect. The side effects of smiling include feeling more relaxed, cool, calm, and being able to think more clearly.

> 'Turn your face to the sun and
> the shadows fall behind you.'
>
> Maori proverb

EXERCISE
Smile therapy

Just test this for yourself when no one is watching: with your eyes open, make a great big fake smile. It doesn't matter whether you show your teeth or not. Just pay attention to your smile, and focus on the area around your mouth as it begins to feel happy. Allow this sensation to spread to your eyes, and notice your whole face relax as your mood begins to lift. Breathe: take deep breaths in through your nose and out through your mouth. Allow the smile to flow through your whole body wherever you most need to relax.

If you want to amplify the effect, laugh out loud to increase the release of endorphins. When you laugh, you take in six times more oxygen than during normal conversation. Laughter adds to the relaxation response by lowering blood pressure and heart rate and also acts like a painkiller by lowering muscle tension. As

*seen in the movie of his book Anatomy of an Illness,
political journalist and professor of humanities Norman
Cousins demonstrated the effectiveness of laughter by
fully recovering from ankylosing spondylitis. When drug
therapy couldn't help him, Cousins left hospital, took
mega doses of vitamin C, and practiced a positive attitude
of love, hope, faith, and laughter. Every day he watched
hours of Marx Brothers movies. He found that 10 minutes
of deep belly laughter had an anesthetic effect that
allowed him to sleep for hours.*[1]

'It is better to laugh at your problems
than to cry about them.'

Jewish proverb

A side benefit of not expressing negative emotions

Psychologists at the University of Cardiff discovered that after people had cosmetic Botox injections, not only could they no longer frown but they also reported feeling happier and less anxious. Curiously this didn't have anything to do with feeling more attractive as a result of the Botox injections, so that didn't explain the emotional lift.[2] Another study at the University of Munich scanned Botox recipients with MRI machines while they were asked to mimic angry faces. They found that the Botox subjects, who couldn't mimic frowns, had much lower activity in the brain circuits involved with emotional processing and responses: the amygdala, hypothalamus, and parts of the brain stem.[3] Scientists are now also studying the effects Botox might have on pain perception.

Children learn by mimicking, matching, and copying everything people say and do around them, including emotional expressions. Throughout life people tend to gravitate toward those who 'match' them. Similarities of behaviors, gestures, use of language, and facial expressions increase feelings of rapport. Try this experiment with a friend: match their facial expressions while they tell an animated story. Most people do this naturally. Then try mismatching with opposite emotions. For example, frown when they smile, or look absent-mindedly out of the window instead of making eye contact. Most people find this exceedingly difficult to do. Meanwhile your friend may find your responses quite weird and disconcerting! Mismatching breaks rapport and gives people the unconscious signal that you are not connecting with them.

Contagious emotions

Emotions and facial expressions are contagious. People unconsciously read the emotions being displayed on other people's faces and respond accordingly. Clinical psychologist Pamela Stephenson noticed her husband Billy Connolly, a well-known UK comedian, and other people close to her began reflecting and responding to the perpetual frown lines she had developed. Because the frown made her look angry, as people unconsciously matched her expression, the mood in the room lowered. So she decided to have some Botox injections to remove the frown lines. To her delight, when everyone reflected her relaxed-looking face, they resonated with her happier feelings.[4]

'Wear a smile and have friends;
wear a scowl and have wrinkles.'
George Eliot

Perhaps you have heard the old saying, 'It takes 43 muscles to frown and only 17 to smile, but it doesn't take any to just sit there with a dumb look on your face.' Different scientists have tried to count the muscles in the face, but this is an inexact science. The numbers of muscles attributed to frowning and smiling vary depending on how you label the muscles. Therefore it seems the old folklore is incorrect. Smiling and frowning both seem to use about the same number of muscles. However that doesn't take into account how much energy each muscle might consume, or which expression has become a habit.

Holding a particular facial expression for only 10 seconds is long enough to produce the associated emotional state. So the mere act of smiling induces happy feelings, just as frowning induces angry feelings. This might be because contracting the facial muscles affects blood flow to the brain. Frowning certainly increases the temperature of the brain, which then releases more neurotransmitters to affect mood. So Mr. Grumpy really is a hothead! Conversely, smiling has associated lower forehead temperatures, literally helping you to keep your cool.

When you walk into the room smiling from the inside out, you radiate sunshine. Happy feelings are so contagious that people will go out of their way to spend more time with you. Unlike the wet blanket who frowns, moans, criticizes and complains, the person with the engaging smile lifts everyone's mood. Such irresistible optimistic rapport breeds cooperation, creativity, and support. Smile and everyone will reflect your smiles back at you.

- What if you smiled before opening your eyes in the morning?
- What if you chose to keep smiling throughout the whole day?
- What if you filled your day with things that make you smile?
- What if you chose something to smile about no matter what?
- What if you could smile even during the most onerous jobs?
- What if you turned around every negative thought with a smile?
- What if you smiled as you turned out the light each night?

The world will seem a much sunnier place when you smile. You will stand taller, sit straighter, and breathe easier. As your body relaxes, any pain you might have will diminish too. When everyone resonates with your smiles, your whole environment will feel more pleasant, healing, and peaceful. Smiling goes well with the Swahili saying *hakuna matata*, which you might know from the story of *The Lion King*. It means 'no worries.' Try adopting this attitude toward any obstacle or difficulty. It is so contagious that everyone in your environment will catch the same cheerful energy too. Such high energy helps solutions emerge naturally, while problems get laughed away. Life feels like an adventure when you pay more attention to the good points and overlook the mistakes.

> *'Happiness does not depend on outward*
> *things, but on the way we see them.'*
> Leo Tolstoy

Creating your future dream

To visualize the creation of your future dream involves willingness and courage. To move toward your dream takes determination and persistence. To manifest your dream into reality requires acceptance and letting go. Whenever you want something in your life, your unconscious mind creates an internal picture of what it will look like. This image gets imbued with all the beliefs and needs you associate with that desire. The positive hope of getting what you want and achieving what you desire will be some form of happiness, fulfillment, success, respect, significance, worthiness, love, certainty or security. Not getting it therefore means the opposite. No one wants disappointing results, so pushing to make things happen seems logical and natural.

Deciding happiness cannot happen until you reach this desired goal in the future prevents success. Unfortunately the more you work toward achieving your goal, the more you perceive it as being separate from you. This increases and energizes the conviction that it hasn't happened yet. That desirable picture is over there, out of reach, probably somewhere in the distant future. Unwittingly this ratifies the fact that you have still to achieve this outcome. You don't have it now; that is a fact. You look around and all evidence confirms this lack in your reality. Simultaneously this verifies other beliefs about the amount of time that might be necessary and particular steps you must take in order to achieve this future desire.

Depending on what beliefs lurk in the cloud of your unconscious, this strategy of moving toward your desired future picture will produce variable results. There are several traps. First, feeling driven to achieve something puts the focus on the future outcome and distracts you from being in the moment. So you become less mindful and more un-centered. The impatience to make things happen turns into tension, pressure, anxiety, stress, and frustration. Hence poor decisions get made because your thinking is hampered by those negative emotions. The inner stress has negative physical effects on the body and reduces your ability to radiate the right energy. Whenever you try to control what happens in the future, you lose control over the present. Plus your desired picture stays firmly stuck in the future, tantalizing you. The temptation is to make comparisons between that future happiness and where you are now. This leads to more negative feelings and more need to chase after the goal with ever-greater determination.

> '*The future ain't what it used to be.*'
> Yogi Berra

The paradox of letting go

Think about what happens when you are in the middle of a problem. What you want to get rid of surrounds you. You feel totally convinced it's real. All your senses confirm multiple kinds of evidence that prove the certainty of its existence, down to the smallest details. You notice what you see, hear, feel, smell, and taste. Maybe you even read verifiable reports that confirm it. The reality of the situation is unquestioned or undoubted. Your sensory experience of it proves the truth of it and your internal dialogue rants and raves about it. You may not like it, but it forms a part of the uncomfortable comfort zone you identify with. You may want something else, but in comparison with this solid reality, that desire feels like mere fantasy. The more you want to get rid of the problem, the more reality it gains.

Do you notice how the strategy of problem behavior is the mirror opposite of wanting to achieve your desired future? The need to chase after the dream you want in the future amplifies the lack: what is unreal cannot be reached. The need to get rid of the problem amplifies the certainty of its existence: what is real does not change. What if it was possible to reverse this process? Before we look into how to do that, you need to check if there is anything you might gain or lose by letting go of what you believe to be true right now. No one holds on to something without good reason.

EXERCISE
Holding on versus letting go

Think of the most important aspects of your future picture. Keep them firmly in mind as you meditate on the following questions to discover all the answers that could be relevant. Ask yourself why this has not yet happened for you. Write your answers down in case you need to work with them later.

◊   *What could you be holding on to?*

◊   *What do you need to let go of?*

◊   *What do you gain by holding on?*

◊   *What could you gain by letting go?*

◊   What could you lose by holding on?

◊   What could you lose by letting go?

◊   What feels crucial about holding on?

◊   What do you fear will happen if you let go?

◊   How do you know if you are still holding on?

◊   How will you know when you have let go?

Your answers should shed some clues about what needs you might unconsciously be trying to satisfy. When a particular goal never gets achieved, there is always a reason. Until you know what that reason might be, there is little choice or possibility of change.

Here are some examples of answers given by a woman who was holding on to her 'desire for a wonderful relationship.' The first question revealed she was holding on to her independence due to insecurity about being valued and significant. She needed to let go of her fear of being controlled, being invisible and her lack of trust, especially around sharing finances. She liked holding on to her freedom and not having to compromise. Conversely if she could let go of her obsessive desire, she would feel less driven, less disappointed, and more peaceful.

Holding on to her desire for a relationship made her needy. Because this needy energy repelled potential partners, she stood less chance of success. This meant she could lose out on love, intimacy, affection, having children and creating a 'home,' as well as opportunities for personal growth and contribution. If she chose to let go of her excessive desire for a relationship, the only things she would lose would *be the needy energy and her excuse for not getting on with life. Holding on to her freedom felt crucial in order to avoid being taken advantage of, cheated, or abused. Her biggest fear was about opening her heart and possibly being rejected or hurt again. Her answers to the questions highlighted many issues in her thought cloud that still needed resolution. She realized that if she continued to hold on to the desire, she just repeated the strategies that never worked. Letting go could free her to relate more authentically to everyone. She could then start enjoying spending time with whomever she was with, and having a good time wherever she was. This motivated her to learn more about how to let go.*

'The question, "What do you want?" must be answered. You are answering it every minute and every second. And each moment of decision is a judgment that is anything but ineffectual. Its effects will follow automatically until the decision is changed.'

A Course in Miracles, Anon

Attachment

Holding on means you have an attachment based on fear, not love. Signs of holding on may show up as feelings of confusion, inertia, frustration, perfectionism, impatience, anxiety, procrastination, or avoidance. Suppressed fear usually leads to activities of compensation: overeating, over-exercising, drinking, drugs, smoking, etc. More subtle forms of attachment occur when you go looking for the solution in all the wrong places. You might think you are doing all the right things, but end up chasing after all the wrong reasons. Track your fear down to its source and capture the precise triggers.

....

EXERCISE
Identify your triggers

◊ *What feeling leads to grasping or trying to control things?*

◊ *What things do you chase: possessions, roles, money, etc.?*

◊ *Who or what need makes you feel clingy and dependent?*

◊ *What is the fear behind whatever you hold on to too tightly?*

◊ *What unresolved memories are being held on to from the past?*

◊ *What drama stories have you been addicted to telling people?*

◊ *What sights, sounds, activities, smells, tastes act as triggers?*

Fear depends on imagining possible negative outcomes. Although it doesn't make sense to do that, the brain's old habits can be hard to break. Attachment and holding on are just signs that old patterns from the past are still in operation. Consider it another invitation to practice your new processes. Instead of remembering, reliving and recreating the past, turn down or switch off the triggers.

....

How can it be possible to let go of what you really want? At first this idea seems counterproductive. It won't work to pretend you no longer want what you really want. And it's equally pointless to pretend you have already let go, when the truth is you're still holding on. You can't kid your mind. Lying to yourself or others simply keeps you stuck. As long as you hold on to your future picture with need, you stay attached. Attachment means trying to be in control, have it your way, force the outcome, assume God's role. Maybe the universe doesn't work according to your plans. Clinging to anything or anyone or any idea indicates some underlying fear.

After hearing my story, people often ask 'Well, Arielle, did you get your perfect partner and the baby you always wanted?' Everyone wants to hear a happy ending. Wouldn't that prove that following these principles produces the desired result? Certainly part of me always hoped so. A part of me wanted to control the outcome, stay attached to my plan and have things my way. But I learned to look deeper. I asked myself why I really wanted to have a baby. For me the answer was about contribution, fulfillment, and giving my love. Of course I could think of many other ways I can contribute and give my love in order to find fulfillment. Looking around I realized at least 50 percent of the population never gives birth, so I let go of being attached to certain aspects of my plan. Instead I focused on how to be more creative, rather than create a baby. After all being able to choose whether or not to have a baby and have a career were choices unavailable to women in previous times. How many of my ancestors might have longed for such an opportunity? Perhaps I owed it to them to make the best of it. Perhaps I owed it to myself to make the best of my life.

The opposite of attachment is to fall in love with where you are right now. Fall in love with what you are doing and experiencing, good or bad. Fall in love with who you are. Imagine you could see yourself through the eyes of the universe. Instead of lack, defects or damaged goods, you look perfect just as you are. Fall in love with being in the moment, enjoying the wonder of everything you experience. Fall in love with doing for doing's sake. Fall in love with the journey instead of the destination. Consider that right here; right now you are in the right place, doing the right thing, even when you make mistakes. Trust everything is all part of a grand plan. Have faith that no matter what happens, it will all work out perfectly.

> *'Be yourself. Everyone else is taken.'*
> Oscar Wilde

Miracle mindfulness

Practicing mindfulness means paying attention with purpose and intent to what is happening in the present moment. It is having acute awareness: direct intuitive knowing what you are doing while you are doing it. That includes knowing what is going on inside your head as well as what is going on in your environment. There is no judgment of the past because the total focus is on being in the present. Instead of allowing the unconscious mind to run movies of old memories, and instead of allowing the conscious mind to control the show by pushing to achieve goals, you just observe. While you watch and respond, you continue participating fully in what's going on.

ACID TEST QUESTION
How do you know if you have let go?

You will know you have let go when it no longer matters whether or not you achieve your goal. You will still desire your future picture, and you will still be doing whatever it takes to help it come about. The big difference will be the lack of urgency and stress. You will feel more calm and centered instead of driven, anxious, or frustrated. Your mind will be quiet and you will feel more like your true self again.

Here are some questions to help you let go of attachment while you hold the intention of your future picture in your mind.

EXERCISE
Let go and enjoy

Think of your future picture and hold it gently in your mind. This is the direction you want to move toward. Do so lovingly, patiently, and with trust. Practice following these suggestions to increase your mindfulness:

◊　*Enjoy the moment, be fully present, experience now.*

◊　*Enjoy each step of the journey as precious.*

◊　*Enjoy whatever you have right now as 'enough.'*

◊　*Enjoy being who you, know you are 'enough.'*

◊　*Enjoy feeling all your feelings, appreciating being alive.*

◊   *Enjoy being an example by giving your gifts, your love.*

◊   *Enjoy accepting and allowing things to be as they are.*

◊   *Enjoy turning things over to your Higher Mind or God.*

◊   *Enjoy being curious about how things will turn out.*

◊   *Enjoy trusting and not knowing how to do everything.*

◊   *Enjoy living your purpose fully in every moment.*

◊   *Enjoy sharing these ideas in order to remind yourself.*

The more you practice entering this state, the more you develop those positive flowing neural pathways in your mind. You will probably start recognizing a few old habitual patterns that try to interrupt. Maybe you can slow them down or stop them altogether. Maybe your new thinking starts to happen naturally as a new habit. You see situations more clearly without the fog of the old thought clouds. Maybe you start responding more effectively and creatively in difficult situations. Maybe you begin to feel more balanced and resilient more of the time. Your body enjoys this peaceful space to relax and put things back to normal.

'Our greatest glory is not in never falling,
but in rising every time we fall.'
Confucius

Just like with meditation, we may experience unwanted thoughts creeping in to intrude on this good space. This is what brains do. How we respond is what counts. If a thought captures our attention and whirls us into a thought cloud, it succeeds in taking us away from the present moment. If we can just acknowledge the thought and let it go without judging it or labeling it a 'failure' then we can retain our focus on the present. When it feels too difficult to stay mindful, we must remember it's just an invitation to do a little more exploration; another gift in disguise!

Instead of revisiting the past, we need to make use of whatever exercises could help to improve our state: 'First aid for stress' (page 73); 'Seven ways to interrupt a thought cloud' (page 143); 'Keep a cool perspective' (page 178); 'Smile therapy' (page 202); 'Let go and enjoy' (page 215); and 'Give yourself permission' (page 225). By refocusing the mind we can turn our attention firmly toward the intended future direction. We can enjoy being in each moment and keep moving toward our desired future picture. Then no matter what happens, we simply accept the feedback, learn the lesson, make the best of it, and see how we can best incorporate it into the journey. Just continue doing whatever it takes, for as long as it takes, remembering to enjoy the journey itself. This positive energy generates great optimism, attracts others to join in and makes it impossible to be defeated. Each step of the journey brings pleasure and success.

Even if things are not perfect yet, we see the perfection in the Divine plan. We wonder what the next step of our development might bring as we appreciate all the benefits of what we have already learned. Our curiosity turns to finding new ways to make the whole process more fun. With great trust in what the future will bring, we feel like celebrating each and every day. Gratitude fills our hearts.

Key points

▶ Both real smiling and fake smiling stimulate happy endorphins.

▶ Happy feelings are so contagious that people will go out of their way to spend more time with you.

▶ Smiling makes you stand taller, sit straighter and breathe easier, and as your body relaxes, any pain will diminish too.

▶ The more you chase a dream, the more you amplify the lack of it.

▶ The more you try to get rid of a problem, the more reality it gains.

▶ Attachment means trying to be in control, having it your way, and forcing the outcome.

▶ The opposite of attachment is to fall in love with where you are, who you are, and what you are experiencing, right now.

▶ You will know you have let go when it no longer matters whether or not you achieve your goal.

··

Choice Thoughts

I enjoy feeling all my feelings, appreciating being alive.

I presuppose empowering meanings behind all events.

My focus is totally on the present, not judging the past.

I am smiling from the inside out and radiating sunshine.

I enjoy whatever I have as enough, knowing I am enough.

As soon as I let go and move on, I can give my best.

Believe something good will come of this, and it will.

Chapter 11

Real-time Resilience

Successful, happy, healthy people don't always have easy, trouble-free lives. In fact most people have to face failures, setbacks, disappointments, and losses. When life throws a challenge in our direction, how easy is it to remember the wisdom we once read in an inspiring book? Even though we may understand the power of thoughts and intentions, how easy is it to forget to turn around our thinking? The mind seems to love churning with judgment, comparisons, criticism, and accompanying negative emotions. People often share these stories in order to get agreement and verification from others. Whenever there is a need to justify our version of reality or have others join in with condemnation, we make being right and being miserable more important than being happy.

Successful people inspire and surprise everyone by transcending impossible obstacles. Instead of being blocked, they enjoy spontaneous remissions, win against the odds, and manifest miraculous results. They seem to live in a different world, one that is blessed with extraordinary luck and good fortune. But does the secret of their success really depend on luck, destiny, or fate? If we look more closely, they have all mastered the important elements of resilience.

During interviews many successful people humbly attribute their good results to luck. They know that telling the truth is simply unpopular. Envious listeners don't want to hear about hard work, determination, persistence, or being able to bounce back when things don't go according to plan. Most listeners want to avoid the effort and responsibility of choosing their thoughts, words, and actions. When they hear about other people succeeding, they feel pressured to raise their game. So putting everything down to luck lets them off the hook. Then they feel no need to make more effort. They can just blame fate and continue to enjoy the laziness of that familiar comfort zone.

One of my friends complained about his bad luck in never being able to find a place to park. He grumbled about crowded streets and made pictures in his mind of no spaces anywhere nearby to park. Unsurprisingly he always experienced exactly what he envisioned. He became so convinced that this was true, he stopped driving anywhere! This sounded very odd to me because the thoughts in my mind were the opposite: I always find parking right in front of wherever I want to go. I imagine the perfect space waiting for me, or someone just about to pull out and leave me that space. This has always worked so well, I have become convinced that my belief is true.

> *'If you always do what you've always done,*
> *you'll always get what you've always got.'*
> Henry Ford

Key elements of resilience

What we believe is possible is the key element for both luck and resilience. Today's fast-paced world demands huge levels of resilience just to cope with all the stress, potential threats, and adversity. People are not born with this trait. Resilience is a by-product of learning and mastering specific skills. Setting good outcomes, despite the risks involved, shows a particular kind of courage. People gain this courage by being aligned with their inner values. Even under stress, they have the self-confidence to continue being highly competent, sure of their ability to cope. They know that if mistakes occur, or if things go wrong, they will recover. The attitude is what makes the difference. They view challenges as growth and development. A mistake provides useful feedback to help them grow smarter and tougher. The strength they acquire then makes it easier to withstand future hardships.

Resilience can be defined as the ability to recover from illness, change, or misfortune. However, the damage must not be too great. When an ecosystem suffers disturbance, given the right factors nature can usually restore the natural balance unless it has gone past a certain threshold. After that it requires a miracle. Of course some problems do look bigger or more difficult than others. So it's surprising to read in *A Course in Miracles*, 'the first thing to remember about miracles is that there is no order of difficulty among them. One isn't harder or bigger than another. They are all the same.' If this is true then a miracle of healing should be as easy as finding a parking space. Certainly people who enjoy spontaneous remissions make it look effortless and quick. However, when we investigate what worked, we find some common patterns. Those miracles involved more than luck or serendipity. Consciously or unconsciously, thoughts shifted, things were forgiven, and significant new choices were made.

Don't overlook the potential energy inherent within a disturbance

When a disturbance significantly interferes with life, energy gets blocked. For those wise enough to listen to the messages of symptoms, identify key elements of a thought cloud and resolve the stuck issues, the energy becomes freely available to transform the disturbance into strength and resilience. This requires accepting what cannot be changed, developing realistic and hopeful new goals and turning losses into opportunities.

Resilience means developing an enduring capacity to cope with stress and adversity. Good coping mechanisms result in being able to bounce back to normal. Building inner strength from facing difficult experiences makes it possible to steel yourself against future stress. This is similar to the way a vaccine inoculation teaches the body to fortify itself against future exposure to disease. An important aspect of coping is how you judge your thoughts, feelings, and actions. Why not give yourself permission to feel what you feel, instead of berating yourself? If you have high expectations or if you tend to be hard on yourself then the following process will definitely help. If you criticize yourself harshly and pepper your speech with 'I should have' or 'I shouldn't have' this is definitely an area for improvement.

> 'And from the midst of cheerless gloom
> I passed to bright unclouded day.'
> Emily Brontë

EXERCISE
Give yourself permission

Capture some of your internal dialogue and listen to how you speak to yourself. What kind of language and voice tone do you hear? Does it sound gentle, loving, understanding, observant, curious, and encouraging? Or does it sound critical, judgmental, harsh, punishing, and mean? How does your internal dialogue make you feel?

1. *Imagine holding all of these thoughts and feelings in a loving non-judgmental way.*

2. *Tune in to your Heart and Higher Mind or ask for help from the Divine or God in rephrasing your internal dialogue. First acknowledge the original statement and then add positive endings to the sentence. Notice that the word 'and' is used instead of 'but.' This small word 'and' opens up possibilities without contradicting currently held beliefs.*

3. *Give yourself permission to have whatever thoughts or feelings you have, and then convert each one from criticism to permission. Start the sentence off and then wait for your Heart to fill in the rest. If you get less than a positive rephrase, first check that it was your Heart talking. Then consider what higher intention could be meant by that answer. Here are some examples:*

I always get it wrong!
◊   *It's okay for me to get it wrong and I am learning to get it right.*

◊ It's okay for me to not get it right and still be a good person.

I shouldn't have done that!

◊ It's okay for me to have made a mistake, and I can correct it.

◊ It's okay for me to make mistakes and do better next time.

Don't be lazy!

◊ It's okay for me to be lazy and still get things done.

◊ It's okay for me to do things in my own time and stay focused.

I'm not good enough!

◊ It's okay for me to be not good enough and still love myself.

◊ It's okay if people think I'm not good enough; I'll still be okay.

It's hopeless, it will never work!

◊ It's okay for me to feel hopeless and trust it can work out perfectly.

◊ It's okay for me to lose hope and look forward to a brighter future.

I just can't do it!

◊ It's okay for me to feel I can't do it, and still have another go.

◊ It's okay for me to feel incapable and continue moving forward.

I don't deserve it!

◊   It's okay for me to feel I don't deserve and be open to the possibility.

◊   It's okay for me to not deserve and still continue giving to others.

Keep rephrasing your internal dialogue until all of your negative feelings dissolve and you feel more at peace. You can use this process every day to clear your state; if the old feelings come back then just give yourself more permission.

The test of your ability to be true to yourself and your commitment to be all you can be is how well you handle situations that used to trigger you. Just be honest with yourself, knowing how you feel inside. Observe how much you have progressed and where there is still room for improvement. No one is perfect. You can't do better than your best.

Sometimes the best you can do is just to contain your feelings, which in itself could be a big step forward. At least you haven't exploded. At least you haven't said something to hurt anyone else. At least you have paused long enough to breathe. Maybe you even remembered to switch into peripheral vision and silently recited your private resilience question. When you transform so much that the same situations no longer trigger the same old response, you are truly victorious. Until then, consider yourself to be a 'work in progress' just like everyone else and know that is okay. Commit to doing your best to walk your talk and continue to practice.

'Hark! I am called. My little spirit, see,
Sits in a foggy cloud and stays for me.'
William Shakespeare, *Macbeth*

Real-time resilience

Real-time computing refers to programs that guarantee a response within a strict time frame, often within milliseconds. It also means that simulations will work as fast as the real thing, or that data will transfer without perceivable delay. If resilience is how well you respond, recover and cope, then real-time resilience means your ability to demonstrate specific skills in every single moment. All the topics discussed throughout the book so far have provided different ways to develop the following six skills of resilience. Master all six skills and it will be easy to make the ultimate choice that heals.

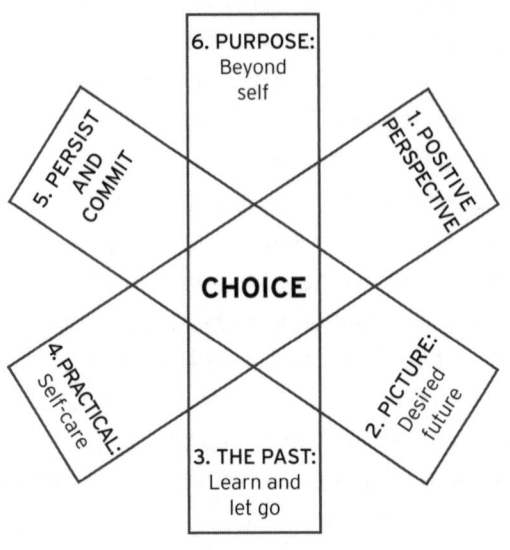

Six skills of resilience

1. Positive perspective

Resilient people rarely waste their time or energy being pessimistic, critical, negative, or complaining. They start with being happy and appreciating what is good already. And it is all good. Regardless of what is happening, they carefully observe, consider all options, and quickly choose positive responses or solutions. Instead of getting hooked on one perspective, instead of insisting on a particular meaning, instead of holding on to some cherished belief, they willingly shift and reframe according to what works best. They keep their focus on higher values.

2. Picture: Desired future

Resilient people know what they want, and they make choices that match their values with ease. Instead of inner conflict, vagueness, or dreams, they know what direction feels right for them. Despite any risks involved, they find it easy to commit when the journey itself feels worthwhile. They have sorted out what is important from what is not. They have resolved inner conflicts and can now harmonize heart, mind, and body toward their desirable perfect future. They are willing to picture this and let it act as a beacon, guiding their path forward.

3 The Past: Learn and let go

Resilient people never lose or fail, they just learn from mistakes and move on. They have processed the stories of their past, resolved their thought clouds, and gained wisdom and compassion. They let go and forgive. They look forward to more growth. When losses occur, they don't crumble. Instead of moaning and feeling sorry for themselves, they look for the upside. What can they do with this? How could this be turned around? What new opportunities could open up as a result? They set new objectives and look forward to new adventurous ways to satisfy their values.

4. Practical: Self-care
Resilient people look after their bodies as well as their minds and feelings. They nourish all parts appropriately: the right amount of healthy food, exercise, rest, sunshine, fun, challenge, and learning. They practice emotional intelligence: they know who they are, honor their feelings, manage their state, listen to the thoughts passing through their mind, motivate themselves and act in alignment with their values. They foster good relationships, showing empathy and enjoying being a part of larger communities. When necessary they accept advice and appropriate treatment.

5. Persist and commit
Resilient people get lucky because they keep on having another go. They just never give up. Instead of becoming discouraged at the first hurdle, they pluck up the courage to keep going. This requires being able to access the right state of mind, manage their emotions, and stay anchored to positive beliefs. They maintain their balance from an inner center of power. Knowing who they are, what is important to them and what they are fully committed to makes it easier for them to negotiate the twists and turns of life. They become adept at managing their energy through mindfulness.

6. Purpose: Beyond self
Resilient people know their life purpose, as well as the values they hold most dear. Privately they express their personal mission, in a statement or a metaphor. They look at the bigger

picture, beyond their own selfish interests. They simply think BIG. Their goals are more ambitious and therefore more motivating and exciting. As it isn't just for them, their success will have a much more profound impact, and will leave a legacy of contribution. When the going gets tough, they find the will to carry on for the benefit of others. Letting others down would mean letting themselves down.

ACID TEST QUESTION
How do I know my resilience has increased?

Collect all your insights, all your answers to the questions, the shifts and changes you have made by doing the exercises throughout this book and you will be well on the way to satisfying each factor of resilience. Then just notice your response to everyday events. Compare that with how you used to react and hopefully you will be pleasantly impressed with your progress.

Isn't it great to be surprised when you thought you already knew everything? If you've done many years of therapy and inner exploration, isn't it a gift when you discover something new? When you stay open-minded and view things from a higher perspective, nothing will ever seem the same again. If a problem still persists, that just means old thought clouds might still be in operation. But don't dismay, just notice every little sign of improvement. Accept it as another invitation to do some more work. True resilience is measured by how you feel inside and how you continue to respond.

What if you could step beyond the usual parameters of your thinking? If you started thinking bigger and bolder and brighter, how different would your future look? If you could be sure of success, what would you do? If you could be sure you would not fail, what would you be willing to do right now? That future you is already beckoning to you, drawing you toward a whole new realm. Instead of throwing away your power, change your thinking. You are free to choose a different path, now and in every moment.

> *'Meditate. Live purely. Be quiet. Do your work with mastery. Like the moon, come out from behind the clouds! Shine.'*
> Buddha

The magic of intention

Prayer, intention, conscious deliberate thinking, and meditation offer effective ways to direct your thought processes for maximum effectiveness. Research undertaken by the PEAR project at Princeton University found that if a large enough group of people meditates together on the same subject, the surrounding society (or field of energy) would be influenced. Statistically, the square root of 1 percent of the overall group's size is all that is needed for this to happen. This means that if 1,732 people focus on the same goal, it could change three million people's minds.[1] Of course the influence of combined thought fields can drive people's energy in either harmonious or disruptive directions.

Prayers enhance your depth of acceptance, appreciation, and gratitude. Appreciation, love and thanks are given for the good that has already been received. The secret is to also give thanks in advance for what has yet to come, as if it has already happened. Just imagine your future picture, adding in all the rich details as if you are experiencing it in the present moment. Hold a vivid picture of celebrating this positive result having already been received, then the love you send will be powerfully multiplied. Time is immaterial. This love travels faster than light, goes any distance and does more good than any other healing technique.

More than 200 healing studies have researched the benefits of prayer. However there are many different ways to pray. Many of the researchers had difficulty defining the type of prayer, the words to use, the length of time spent praying, the number of repetitions, and how much passionate energy should be involved. That may explain why the results of these studies were variable, yet 75 percent of the studies showed positive benefits.[2] Confident expectancy and gratitude coupled with intense desire evokes a powerful energy. Needy begging prayers coupled with a sense of lack and hopelessness have completely different energy. When praying for others, how the prayer might be received needs to be carefully taken into consideration if they know you are praying for them. If someone says they are praying for you, do you take that as a positive loving intention or do you interpret their prayers to mean they think the situation is a lost cause and nothing else will work?

The most vital ingredients for healing prayers are focus and letting go. Have a clear and intense focus: see your future picture already happening all around you, filling your senses. Allow that energy to expand up into the universe; let it go out into the Field, or turn it over to God. The words used are less important than the quality of intense attention, expansion and letting go. Such spiritual practices soothe the heart rhythms, slow down the breathing, and steady the brain wave patterns.

No wonder such practices are common to every religion, spiritual path and shamanic tradition throughout history. Not only do they access the wisdom of the Higher Mind, but they also help to restore health.

When meditation and prayer are done in groups, the positive effect is greatly multiplied. I experienced this kind of support during my long healing journey, when one of my dear friends organized her prayer group to include me in its weekly prayers. I chose to receive these prayers by feeling honored and touched that a group of complete strangers would think of me and send their love and positive energy from the other side of the world. My heart is still full of gratitude for their loving prayers that surely helped my healing process.

'What lies behind us and lies before us are small matters compared to what lies within us. And when we bring what is within us out into the world, miracles happen.'
Henry David Thoreau

The positive benefits of meditation have also been thoroughly researched, especially by the Maharishi Yogi Foundation. Many of their studies have shown that when only 1 percent of the population of a city practices regular 'transcendental meditation' techniques, the crime rate in that city goes down by 22 percent. They predict that 1 percent of the world's population would be enough to influence the whole world. The size of the group may be less important than the intensity of the meditative focus.[3] In order to build resilient brain waves that are in sync with your heart, you need to build the congruence that comes from practice.

The Institute of HeartMath in California published surprising results about the extensive measurements of the electrical fields of the body. The heart's electrical field is about 60 times greater in amplitude than that of the brain and this can be measured anywhere on the body using an electrocardiogram (ECG). The electromagnetic frequency (EMF) of the heart measured 5,000 times stronger than the field generated by the brain. The heart's frequencies can be measured by a SQUID-based magnetometer reaching as far as 25ft (7.5m) from the body, while those of the brain fade out at 1ft (30.5cm). Every time the heart beats, it creates a pressure wave, felt throughout the body. The heart acts as a global synchronizing system by sending drumbeat signals all through the body. Each beat of the heart sends messages to every body cell. Other hearts will also resonate with the strongest vibrations.[4] Could this explain why feelings are so contagious? Like musical instruments, we vibrate and resonate with other people's drumbeats.

The whole body receives the benefits when the heart resonates with the right kind of intention energy. Just saying one little prayer won't have much effect if the rest of the day is filled with angst, but at least it's a start. As you transform all the old ideas and beliefs in your old thought cloud, you can build a new cloud of positive thoughts, prayers and energy. Amplify this with more consistent practice, until everything you do becomes infused with your positive intention.

Love will immediately enter into
any mind that truly wants it.
A Course in Miracles, Anon

Community of saints

Have you ever stopped to think about all the people who have positively sponsored you in your life? Think about the people in the past who have always believed in you, and saw you for who you really are. Who supported you or stood up for you? Who nourished your development and encouraged you? These are the people Carl Jung would have called your 'community of saints.' They were the allies you could depend on. Parents and families often filled that role, but there may also have been teachers, friends, or colleagues who did even more. Who has acted as an angel in your life, helping you when you needed it the most?

Who sponsors you now? Who might be wishing you well and sending you prayers right now? Perhaps it is time to acknowledge and thank whoever is a member of your healing support team. Know whom you can turn to for encouragement and backup. Treasure the team of angels who guard your back. Who listens, respects you and gives you the space to learn and do whatever you need to do at your own pace? Your angels may include family members, friends, colleagues, teachers, doctors, therapists, and gurus, even people you have only met in books. Each one may supply different kinds of assistance at different times. New people may suddenly appear and play an important role for a short time. After performing that specific purpose they might disappear again. Be curious to meet the angels who show up for you.

Have you ever stopped to think that everything in life comes to you through relationships with others? Since the day you were born, your life has depended on people taking care of you. Even your conception required two people. Throughout childhood and school, people acted as guides and teachers.

You may have had role models or people you emulated. Every action, every job involves some kind of communication with others. Even working alone at a computer must eventually require some interaction with other people. No one is an island. Everyone is connected. Therefore your health, fulfillment, happiness, financial success, in everything you do, depends on your ability to interact well with others. How well you interact with others reflects how you treat yourself.

> '*A sorrow shared is half the sorrow.*
> *A joy shared is twice the joy.*'
> Jewish proverb

Loving yourself

How well do you sponsor yourself? What does it mean to love yourself? Does it mean indulging yourself with your favorite things: food, chocolate, bubble baths, or sweet treats? That would be a big improvement instead of berating yourself, but it is only a start. Think about how you might give your love to a child or pet. Surely love would mean providing a health-promoting proper diet, not just candies. You would speak gently to them, teaching by encouragement and examples. You would show endless patience and not punish them for making mistakes. You would reward them when they win and celebrate their successes. You would empathize with their feelings, take interest in what they do and show support and concern when they faltered. You would trust in their ability to find their own solutions, and give assistance only when necessary. You would focus on strengths and overlook deficiencies. You would stand up for them, be there for them, protect them and keep them safe. Your genuine care would be on call any time it was needed. You would make their happiness your priority.

Imagine how good it would feel to have someone love you like that. Someone you could really count on, who is always there for you. Someone you totally trust, who would never let you down. Someone who overlooks mistakes as unimportant and loves you so much they hang in there until a solution is found. Imagine walking hand in hand through life with such an incredible friend, knowing that love will always be by your side giving you inner strength.

How well do you love and sponsor yourself in these ways? By giving yourself such loving support, the same will be mirrored by others. Consider becoming the most important member of your support team. Being an angel to yourself will require making friends with your unconscious mind and your conscious Higher Mind. Through meditation, inner exploration, listening within and being mindful, you can build cooperation and rapport. You become one aligned self, whole and complete. Then the perfection of the path you have been traveling so far will open to reveal even more delights to come.

Key points

▶ Mistakes provide useful feedback to help you grow smarter and tougher, making it easier to withstand future hardships.

▶ When an ecosystem suffers disturbance, given the right factors nature can usually restore the natural balance.

▶ Resilience means developing an enduring capacity to cope with stress and adversity.

- Prayer and meditation effectively soothe the heart rhythms, slow down the breathing, and steady the brain wave patterns.

- The heart acts as a global synchronizing signaling system in the body, coordinating the 80 trillion cells.

- The positive effect of meditation and prayer is greatly multiplied when practiced in groups.

- Prayers enhance the depth of acceptance, appreciation, and gratitude for the good that has already been received.

- People who have positively sponsored you and believed in you might be sending you prayers right now.

Choice Thoughts

I have the courage to keep going and never give up.

I maintain my balance from an inner center of power.

I learn from mistakes and move on, letting go and forgiving,

I listen to my heart, knowing I cannot do
better than my best.

I give thanks for the good that has already been received.

I also give thanks in advance for what
has not yet happened.

I make happiness my priority and I choose peace.

Chapter 12

The Choice that Heals

The choices you make reveal a great deal about who you think you are. Your concept of identity is key to this whole process. The jolts of life force you to wake up, re-evaluate what's important, and question the meaning of life. Who is the self who experiences these thoughts, desires, feelings, and memories? Exploring what has been stored on the shelves lining the walls of your thought cloud is like searching the dark corners of the attic with a flashlight. As you shine the light around, it reveals lots of dusty old objects stored there a long time ago, but it does not reveal who is holding the flashlight. When you look within, you become aware of ideas, images, thoughts, and feelings but not who you are.

The true sense of self can't be seen because what is doing the experiencing is the energy that is you. This true self is easily overlooked and taken for granted because the everyday conscious self makes so much noise focusing on all those ideas, thoughts and feelings. The clamoring of the conscious everyday ego needs, desires, and objectives tends to drown out the soft voice of your true self. So in order to listen to your true self, you need to be quiet.

The ultimate spiritual quest is to know who you are and to liberate yourself. Is it possible to live in the virtual reality created by your mind without being seduced into believing it is real? Throughout time people have searched for ways to access the true self, describing it as being outside, above, and beyond the body. People naturally equate looking up with what is higher, more important, and more spiritual. So it's easy to conclude that the true self is somewhere above you, separate, distant, invisible, and intangible. Connecting with this Higher Self requires special effort so it seems less attainable and too difficult to reach.

Meanwhile the conscious self has no trouble convincing you that the daily affairs of getting those needs met are a very real and important business. The evidence of your environment surrounds you. Your senses constantly relay messages about what look like lumps of very solid matter all around you. What you seem to see, hear, feel, smell, and taste easily persuades you into believing the reality of your senses. When you feel hunger and pain, the body feels very real. So the truth about those questionable sensory perceptions and the power of your true self get forgotten.

'*Beyond the mountains there are mountains again.*'
Haitian proverb

The power of your intentions

As discussed in the previous chapter, the Institute of HeartMath in California has undertaken some interesting experiments, and they also teach specific tools for balancing heart-rhythm patterns. When the heart wave rhythms become regular, smooth and in sync they are called coherent. High coherence is associated with lower stress levels, higher energy levels and the ability of the heart and the brain to work together for optimal clarity, perception and performance. HeartMath performed some fascinating experiments that illustrate the power of intentions. First, they trained 28 researchers how to generate coherent heart waves by governing their thoughts and feelings through breathing and special practices such as meditation. Then each was handed a vial containing human placental DNA. They were instructed to beam strong feelings of gratitude, love, and appreciation toward the vial. Measurements showed that the DNA responded by relaxing until the strands unwound. The length of the DNA became longer. However, when the researchers were instructed to feel anger, fear, frustration, or stress, the DNA responded by tightening up, becoming shorter, and switching off many of the regulatory sequence codes. These experiments demonstrate the immediate connection between mind and body. Stressful feelings from the conscious mind cause the DNA in cells to tighten and shorten, while the consequence of feeling love and appreciation from the true self relaxes and opens it.[1]

To heal means to achieve a state of natural balance. This describes a continuous dynamic process rather than an end result. Each feeling, each breath, each choice, each change in biochemistry, each shift of DNA are like musical chords being played by both mind and body. Moment by moment the different energies interact and counteract, freely improvising the spontaneous jazz of your identity. The same composition is never played exactly the same way twice. The interplay of chaos and order, like the balance of yin and yang energies, forms a never-ending dynamic flow. There is no end state. Nothing is finite. Everything in nature, everything throughout the universe, is part of a vast interconnected energy dynamic. Like a giant hologram, even the smallest parts reflect the whole. Every part is just as important as every other part. Nothing is separate or permanent.

> *'When the music changes, so does the dance.'*
> African proverb

Answers to the common questions people ask

The path to creating lasting positive change rarely goes in a straight line. Every journey follows a zigzag path. Energy travels unpredictable routes. Because everything flows in a continuous state of flux, staying flexible is key. Resolving a problem may be complicated when the issues are multifaceted. The solutions need to be fluid, dynamic, and robust. It's your answers to the questions posed throughout this book that will help you navigate your way.

When you have the necessary clarity about your direction and purpose, when you identify what blocks you, when you resolve what used to keep you stuck, then you can free up the energy and naturally attract the solutions you truly want. As a summary of what has been covered, here are some answers to those questions people commonly ask:

▶ How can I make a miracle happen when I need one?

▶ How could this have happened to me, and why now?

- How is it possible that my thoughts have contributed to this?

- How can I resolve this problem and get rid of it now?

- How is it possible to forgive what is unforgivable or let go?

- How can I bounce back and prevent it from happening again?

How can I make a miracle happen when I need one?

Wanting to make a miracle happen sounds positive. First you need to get clear on what kind of miracle you want. That means answering the most difficult question of all: what do you really want? How you describe that desired goal to yourself, and how you talk about it to others, reveals what kind of energy fuels that desire. Are you moving away from what you don't want in fear, or are you moving toward what is positive and brings joy? When your goal is fully aligned with who you are, whom you came to be, and where you want to go, then you are more than halfway to manifesting a miracle. Need is the antithesis of trusting and allowing. Need breeds attachment. Let go of any neediness or attachment. Cultivate a positive expectancy instead of having expectations. A better question to ask yourself would be: *Am I willing to do whatever it takes, for as long as it takes, to manifest what I want?*

How could this have happened to me, and why now?

Instead of feeling sorry for yourself, take responsibility. How much you accept responsibility equals how much power you have to make changes. Let go of wondering why you deserved this. Be curious to find out how this could be the best thing to have happened. Instead of looking for where to put the blame, choose to be responsible for what happens next. Use your energy to get clear about what you truly want. In which direction do you want to move? What positive purpose could unfold? Instead of focusing on bad timing, trust that what's happening now is perfect. Remember, you can't change the past; you can only change how you think in the present moment. Heal the thoughts here and now and commit to improving things for the future. Let go of any temptation to think you have been specially selected for punishment. A better question to ask yourself would be: *How can I accept and learn from what has happened, and move on?*

How is it possible that my thoughts have contributed to this?

Your conscious thoughts occupy less than 10 percent of your mind. By definition you cannot be conscious of what is unconscious. As it would be crazy to deliberately create problems, it must be your unconscious thoughts doing this, not your conscious thoughts. Learn how to tune in to these inner workings of your mind. The 60,000 thoughts per day you have been thinking for many years have contributed to where you are right now. Whatever you are experiencing in your mind right now, is what you put there in the past. How you are thinking now creates where you will be tomorrow. So if you are unhappy where you are, change how you think. Your conscious and unconscious mind both use the same brain cells. All it takes is a little focused practice to direct your attention to more positive thoughts. A better question to ask yourself would be: *How do I need to think differently in order to manifest the miracles I want?*

How can I resolve this problem and get rid of it right now?

Getting rid of your problem sounds like a good idea until you realize that it involves self-attack. Because part of your mind created this problem, it belongs to you... Just as you wouldn't want to get rid of your left leg, your phone, or your credit card, it's not advisable to get rid of your problem until you understand why you invited it in. Appreciate how this problem has been useful. Be grateful for the ways it has served you. Start accepting all the good benefits you have gained by having this problem. What do you not have to do? What do you get to avoid? The need to get rid of it merely intensifies its reality. Let go and make friends with it instead and feel instant peace. A better question to ask yourself would be: *What helps me remember I am always okay and I can continue to learn whatever I need to become even better?*

How is it possible to ever forgive the unforgivable and let go?

Learn the secret of how to look at things from other perspectives, so you can tap into alternative thinking to transform how you view the issue. Then change outmoded beliefs, reassess what is most important to you, let go of negative emotions, heal the past, and access the wisdom of your Higher Mind. After you rediscover what is true for you, forgiveness makes more sense. After you understand the positive intentions involved, and appreciate how you have learned from making your mistakes, you may be surprised to discover that most things can be forgiven. It's not about condoning bad behavior. Holding on to the need to punish, get revenge, or remember wrongs keeps you stuck. Forgiveness sets you free. A better question to ask would be: *Looking at this through eyes of love, how different would it feel and what could I let go of right now?*

How can I bounce back and prevent it happening again?

Lasting change starts with aligning yourself with what is true – what you stand for, what you value, and how you give your gifts are all ways of loving yourself. Align these and your energy bounces back naturally. You can only genuinely love others to the degree you already love yourself. However it never hurts to practice giving your love anywhere, anytime. Be generous with your smiles and positive energy. As you heal the past and stop repeating old behavior patterns, you also become more resilient. Not reacting to old triggers prevents old thought clouds from rolling in to obscure your thinking again. Then the sunshine of your positive energy can attract what you really want. A better question to ask would be: *How can I deflect the old triggers, turn my thoughts around instantly, and focus on the positive?*

> 'The miracle comes quietly into the mind
> that stops an instant and is still.'
> *A Course in Miracles*, Anon

Remember, you cannot change what you are not aware of... You cannot achieve objectives if you are obsessively attached to the outcome. You cannot let go if you are fiercely holding on. You cannot reach inner serenity until you reconnect with your true inner self. As soon as you connect with your inner light, peace reigns, everything makes sense, conflicts cease, problems evaporate, and healing occurs. Just choose to have thoughts of gratitude for everything, trusting that whatever may not look so bright at the moment, sooner or later will be revealed as a blessing.

....

EXERCISE
Questions to stay on track

◊   *What could I do today to move me toward what I want?*

◊   *How can I make sure I don't settle for my comfort zone?*

◊   *What will help me stay aligned with my true purpose?*

◊   *How can I be more open to receive my desirable future?*

◊   *What can I presuppose to be true that makes me smile?*

◊   *How would the person I want to become think and behave?*

◊   *What will help me let go, accept, and remember to trust?*

....

The choice that heals

Until the mind has been trained to think differently, old habits will continue to direct our energy. How we react and respond, how we express or suppress our emotions will follow pre-existing decisions and beliefs. These loops of repetitive thoughts will result in habitual behaviors. Stress will stimulate the adrenals to release hormones into the body, raising blood pressure, increasing heart rate, diverting brain activity to fight or flight, shutting down rational thought, halting digestion and tensing muscles, etc. Long-term stress accumulates in the body, causing wear and tear until organs weaken and problems occur.

A better choice is to learn how to manage your mind and emotions. Simple interventions like pausing, breathing and reflecting before you speak buy you crucial moments of clear thinking. Stopping to consider different perspectives helps you stay calm and interpret the event with compassion. You weigh up your options looking for what best fits your true identity and purpose. You presuppose that no matter what has occurred, things happen for a reason. Your internal dialogue uses supportive and encouraging words, while you remember to ask your personal resilience question. You may notice that what has occurred mirrors some of your deeper behaviors. So you welcome further opportunities to grow and heal some more.

> '*Can't you see the angel imprisoned in the block of stone trying to get out? I am trying to free him.*'
> Michelangelo

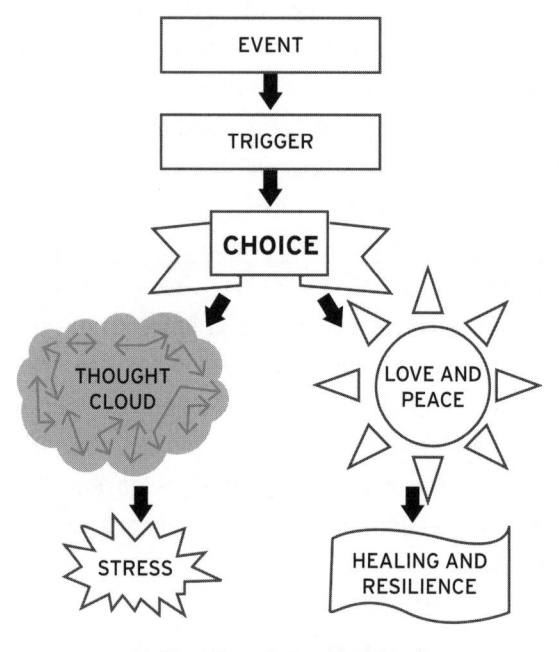

Making the choice that heals

When facing a challenging situation, or a significant emotional event, the ultimate 'choice' is simple: you can either allow the old stress loops to kick into play or you can practice new ways of thinking. This is your moment; the 'choice' that heals. As a significant 'event' occurs, certain aspects will act as 'triggers.' The heart and the body's sensory apparatus immediately respond, sending signals to the brain. How you then interpret the situation makes all the difference. Will you fall into past programming and become immersed in the cloud or will you choose new pathways of thinking? What will you choose? How you rationalize the sensations and emotions depends on what you decide they mean. At this point you have the free will to make a conscious choice.

If you allow the old triggers to suck you into the vortex of the thought cloud, you will become embroiled in the usual familiar turmoil. The old neural pathways will spin you around in endless loops of thinking, beliefs and mistakes of the past. Negative emotions and stress will result, taking their toll on your body. This is the path of dis-ease.

The positive choice means you pause just long enough to take a breath, switch into peripheral vision, and ask yourself your special resilience question and smile from your heart. That crucial moment allows you to stay calm and remember what is really important to you. Guided by your purpose, your true self chooses 'love and peace.' Happiness and positive energy flow through your body releasing all the right hormones for 'healing' and lasting 'resilience.' How could it be any easier?

> *'There is really nothing you must be.*
> *And there is nothing you must do.*
> *There is really nothing you must have.*
> *And there is nothing you must know.*
> *There is really nothing you must become.*
> *However, it helps to understand that fire burns,*
> *and when it rains, the earth gets wet.'*
> Japanese Zen scroll

One day while walking through London, my overactive mind was enjoying running some old depressing thoughts. As I rounded a corner, I saw a fellow sitting on the pavement chanting 'Change please, change please, change please.' I thought to myself: *What profound wisdom! He is giving me a message from the universe!* As he helped me remember I had the power to make a new choice, change my thoughts and my life, my heart filled with gratitude and a sense of connectedness.

Desire is a beautiful thing

A flower turns to face the sun because it naturally seeks the nourishment of light and because it feels good. Seeking what feels natural and good works. The secret of making a good choice is learning to be happy *before* you get what you want. The positive aspect of not having everything you want is getting to feel desire and anticipation. Have you ever noticed that as soon as you succeed in getting what you want, the pleasure fades quite quickly? You think of something else very soon. The brain is wired to always want more. Not having everything you want is good because it keeps you motivated. Enjoy being in the state of expectancy. Know there are always more good things to come. As soon as you stop struggling to get somewhere, you will be carried along effortlessly by the current of life, toward what is true for you.

The power of your positive thinking is about 10,000 times more powerful than your negative thinking. So setting your positive desire with all your heart is the easier choice. Just remember to let go. That doesn't mean sitting around all day doing nothing, although lots of laughing Buddhas do. The trick is to turn what you think you have to do into enjoying the privilege of what you get to do. Lucky you! The instant you catch yourself thinking you have to be doing something, change that thought. Make everything an adventure of discovery instead. What amazing things do you get to experience next? Make everything a choice filled with joy, curiosity and wonder. No matter what happens, *hakuna matata*, no worries, you are free.

'When you realize how perfect everything is you will tilt your head back and laugh at the sky.'
Buddha

....

EXERCISE
Let feelings be your guide

When you need guidance from your true self, just tune in to your feelings. Become aware of the subtle messages being conveyed to you. A simple way to receive guidance from your feelings is to pay attention to your breathing. Place your hand on your belly wherever you can feel movement as you breathe in and out. Then think of choices you could make; for example, think of two different vacation destinations. Just imagine one choice in full detail: how it looks, sounds, and feels. Notice how your breathing feels. Then imagine the other choice and notice how your breathing changes or feels different. This subtle shift in your breathing reveals your preference.

If this is too vague, try the same experiment with two different people: one you like very much and another who you find difficult. Think of each one and pay attention to any shift in your breathing. Note the difference. This can be extremely useful for making all kinds of decisions and choices. Even choosing your food from a menu in a restaurant. Don't be swept away by seductive desires. If you ask, your true self will quietly let you know what is right for you.

....

'Be thou the rainbow in the storms of life.
The evening beam that smiles the clouds away,
and tints tomorrow with prophetic ray.'

Lord Byron

Practical Miracles

The neurons in the inner sky of your mind are twinkling like trillions of stars, waiting for you to make a wish. The most important aspect about making choices is keeping yourself out of the way. Having fewer thought clouds cluttering up your horizon means a clear sky, open for whatever you want to choose. The work on those old issues in the thought clouds needs to be done. But life will always be about 'work in progress,' not reaching perfection. You are already perfect in your imperfection. As long as you are still alive in a body, your journey and your mission are not over. Perhaps the work will never be complete.

Every challenge brings extraordinary gifts. Instead of looking for what is wrong, look for what is right and you will always find it. *Practical Miracles* of healing have little to do with physical treatments and everything to do with shifting your perception. Shifting your consciousness away from the past frees you to live more fully in the present and move toward the future in a joyous state of expectancy.

Practical enlightenment means letting go of fear and embracing whatever happens in your life with love. When you just do what you can with what you have, it will always be enough. Ultimately, miracles don't matter at all, because it is love and the source of love that are important. So just choose to focus on what is good... and it is all good.

....

Choice Thoughts

My healing is a continuous dynamic process.

I let go of expectations and enjoy a constant
state of expectancy.

I am willing to do whatever it takes, for as long as it takes.

My positive feelings let me know what is true for me.

Healing my thoughts now will affect what
happens in the future.

My positive future beckons to me, drawing me forward.

When I connect with my true inner self, I feel at peace.

I appreciate what is good... and it is all good.

Afterword

The choice we make in each moment is the key. By exercising our free will, we wield unbelievable power to influence, if not create the reality around us. Each choice reflects our sense of identity: who we think we are, what we believe to be our purpose. This sense of self isn't a limitation but a springboard. Every starting point is perfect. It's our choice whether to dive in or hesitate. Sometimes we jump for joy and sometimes we fall down. Just as in nature sometimes we choose to create and sometimes we need to destroy in order to clear the way for rebirth. No matter what happens we can choose to be tough and resilient. Like nature, we can bounce back.

How we choose to evolve, how fast we grow, how much we dare to change, all shape the stories that unfold. Each story details a hero's journey of challenges conquered, obstacles overcome, and problems defeated. These never-ending stories mirror the richness of possibilities and probabilities available throughout the universe. Infinite variety, infinite selection, and infinite choices abound. To choose well requires us to be fully present, in the moment of now. Like spiritual gurus we need to learn how to pay attention and not be seduced by appearances. What seems to be real may look very different when our attention shifts into a softer focus of love. When we direct our attention to the consciousness that is doing the seeing instead of the objects that appear in our vision, we make better use of our senses.

When we raise our awareness we begin to understand that we are not separate individual beings struggling for survival, but part of the vast hologram interwoven with all that is. The 80 trillion cells that make up our bodies show us what is possible. From the moment of our conception, our cells face limitless choices about how to differentiate, grow and multiply in completely different and unique ways. Each one is a microscopic world of activity, full of tiny organelles doing zillions of tasks. Within the scope of their destiny – probably dictated by the blueprint of DNA and the Field – these cells still have choices to make. They must respond to whatever happens in their environment. Mistakes occur and problems must be rectified. Yet these miraculous little cells never act like separate entities struggling to survive. They are not competing with each other or trashing their environment. They cooperate on a grand scale, working together with all the other cells. They constantly communicate with every other part of the body. Their coordinated efforts create something far bigger and far grander than anything any one of them could individually imagine. When each cell is healthy and functioning well, their cooperative strength is virtually invincible. The body they help to create is a walking miracle.

Like a body cell, each of us needs to make sure that our unit of identity is intact, healthy, and functioning well. Health-minded individuals working cooperatively together create miracles. When we know who we are and where we fit, our joining with others creates strong bonds. When we respond appropriately to our environment, our solutions help everyone. When we are vigilant in our mindfulness, our presence becomes meaningful. When we take responsibility for our patch, our collective power multiplies. When we allow Grace to guide our choices, our miracle-mindedness becomes an invincible force.

When cells in one part of the body lose their battles, malfunction, or perish, all the other cells are at risk. Their cooperative and frantic efforts to restore natural order may or may not be enough to keep the body alive. Yet even at the last moment, after devastating destruction, after everyone has given up and lost hope, spontaneous remissions occur. A miracle happens. The damage heals. It's not too late. Maybe it's never too late. Maybe natural order can be restored to the whole ecosystem. But we must not waste any more time. We need to take the responsibility to make the choices that heal ourselves first. Then our combined and coherent consciousness has more chance to turn things around.

A Practical Miracle means nothing more than choosing better thoughts and nothing less than knowing there were no mistakes. Past mistakes that have been processed and forgiven provide precious learning. The practical part always involves forgiveness. When we choose to forgive fully, eventually we reach the place of knowing there was nothing to forgive. When we choose to heal, eventually we remember that in our essence, there was nothing wrong. We are more than just physical bodies. Healing is wholeness. When we choose to remember who we really are, there is nothing but magnificence all along.

Perhaps there are no finite endings, only more beginnings. We can only start from where we are now and make better choices about where we want to go. We have friends in high places. Whenever we choose with love, we join with the creative forces of the whole universe. The better we align with our energies, the more that will be mirrored in the energies of our environment. Our thoughts can heal the world. We need to let go of the idea that we are separate. True resilience is built on trust and faith. We need to look beyond the limitations of our sensory awareness and connect with all that is. Then we can do better than our best.

Hopefully we will all learn to do better at accepting our power. When we remember to use our consciousness to visualize, there are no limits to the good we can bring into being. Please remember to smile, breathe deeply, and enjoy every moment!

Endnotes

Introduction

1. McTaggart, L. 'The 8 Mental & Emotional Changes Associated with Spontaneous Remissions,' *What Doctors Don't Tell You*; February 2009; 19(11); 9. Quoted with kind permission from Lynne McTaggart

Chapter 1: How Can You Make a Miracle Happen When You Need One?

1. Lipton, B. *The Biology of Belief* (Elite Books, 2005); 140-4
2. Fraser, P. and Massey, H. *The Living Matrix* (Institute of Noetic Science; 13 March 2009)
3. Moseley, J.B., O'Malley K., *et al*. 'A Controlled Trial of Arthroscopic Surgery for Osteoarthritis of the Knee,' *'New England Journal of Medicine*; 2002; 347(2); 81-8

Chapter 2: Mental Medicine: Healing the Heart of the Mind

1. Ziglar, Z. 'The Legendary Story of Major James Nesbeth,' *See You at the Top* (Pelican, 2000)

Chapter 3: Why Has This Happened and Why Now?

1. Lipton, B. *The Biology of Belief* (Elite Books, 2005); 62, 65, 66, 72)

2. Fraser, P. and Massey, H. *The Living Matrix* (Institute of Noetic Science, 13 March 2009)

3. Fraser, P. and Massey, H. *The Unturned Stone* (Nutri-Energetics Systems Ltd, 2006)

4. Cairns, J., Overbaugh, J. and Millar, S. *The Origin of Mutants* (Nature Publishing; Dept. of Cancer Biology, Harvard School of Public Health, 1988)

5. Chopra, D. 'Replacement of Body Cells,' *Quantum Healing* (Bantam, 1990)

6. Lipton, B. and Bhaerman, S. 'Multiple Personalities,' *Spontaneous Evolution* (Hay House, 2011)

7. Pribrum, K. 'Holographic Brain Theory,' *Brain and Behaviour* (Penguin, 1969)

8. 'Babies Learning to See' (National Science and Technology Council, Social, Behavioural and Economic Research in the Federal Context, January 2009)

9. Darwin, C. 'Santa Cruz, Patagonia, and the Falkland Islands,' *The Voyage of the Beagle* (Journal and Remarks, Henry Colburn of London, 1839)

10. Lipton, B. and Bhaerman, S. 'Brain Programmed for Negative Thoughts, Brain Waves,' *Spontaneous Evolution* (Hay House, 2011)

11. Worth, K. 'How Children's Brains Learn and Build Thought Structures,' *The Power of Children's Thinking* (Natural Science Foundation, 2000); www.nsf.gov/pubs/2000/nsf99148/ch_4.htm

12. Doidge, N. 'Reliving memories,' *The Brain that Changes Itself* (Penguin, 2008)

13. Marilyn Schlitz lecture 'Brain Builds Structures,' Institute of Noetic Science, London, 2011

14. Dunning, D. and Kruger, J. 'Not Knowing What We Don't Know,' 'Unskilled and Unaware of It,' 'How Difficulties of Recognizing One's Own Incompetence Leads to Inflated Self-assessments,' *Journal of Personality and Social Psychology*; 1999; 77(6); 1121–1134

Chapter 4: Mindfulness: The Key Resource of Resilience

1. Erickson, M. *My Voice Will Go With You* (W. W. Norton, 1982)
2. Sperry, R. 'Brain Lateralization: Consciousness, Personal Identity and the Divided Brain,' *Neuropsychologia*; 1984: 22(6); 661-673

Chapter 5: How Does Thinking Create Stress?

1. Fraser, P. and Massey, H. *The Living Matrix* (Institute of Noetic Science, 13 March 2009)
2. Janoff-Bulman, R. and Hanson Frieze, I. 'Victims: 3 Sources of Distress, A Theoretical Perspective for Understanding Reactions to Victimization,' *Journal of Social Issues:* 1983; 39(2); 1-17
3. Campbell, J. 'Hero's Journey, External, Internal, Intimate Forces,' *The Hero with a Thousand Faces* (New World Library, 2008)

Chapter 8: Cloudy With a Chance of Scattered Miracles

1. Sheldrake, R. 'Sense of Being Stared At,' *The Sense of Being Stared At and Other Aspects of the Extended Mind* (Arrow, 2004)
2. Samanta-Laughton, M. 'Entanglement: Punk Science,' *Inside the Mind of God* (John Hunt Publishing, 2006)
3. 'Fraser, P. and Massey, H. *The Living Matrix* (Institute of Noetic Science, 13 March 2009)
4. McTaggart. L, *The Field* (Element Books, 2001)
5. McTaggart. L, *The Intention Experiment* (Harper Element, 2008)

Chapter 10: Fly above the Clouds

1. Cousins, N. *Anatomy of an Illness* (Bantam, 1998)
2. Lewis, M. 'Injecting Cosmetic Happiness,' *Botox: News Centre University of Cardiff*; April 2009

3. Wenner, M. 'Smile, It Could Make You Happier,' *Botox: Scientific American*; October 2009

4. Hardy, R. 'Pamela Stephenson: To hell with beige stretch trousers – while you've got it, flaunt it,' *Mail Online*, 3 February 2012

Chapter 11: Real-time Resilience

1. Nelson, R. 'Meditation: Global Consciousness Project,' PEAR, Princeton University, 1998; http://noosphere.princeton.edu/science2.html

2. McTaggart. L, ' Prayer and Meditation,' *The Intention Experiment* (Harper Element, 2008)

3. Hagelin, J.S. *et al.* 'Transcendental Meditation: Effects of Group Practice of TM program on preventing violent crime in Washington,' November 1998

4. McCraty, R., Tiller, W., Atkinson, M. 'Measurements of Heart and Brain: HeartMath,' 'Science of the Heart: Exploring the Role of the Heart in Human Performance;' http://www.heartmath.org/research/research-library/research-library.html

Chapter 12: The Choice that Heals

1. McCraty, R., Tiller, W., Atkinson, M., 'Coherence of Heart: HeartMath,' 'Science of the Heart: Exploring the Role of the Heart in Human Performance' and 'You can heal your DNA;' http://www.heartmath.org/research/research-library/research-library.html

Resources and Recommended Reading

To assist you on your healing journey here is a list of books you might find particularly informative and inspiring. Many of these have become 'classics' and provided some of the insights in this book.

Communication and consciousness

Ask and It Is Given, Esther and Jerry Hicks (Hay House, 2005): An essential book on emotions and manifesting; great techniques and explanations.

Blink, Malcolm Gladwell (Penguin, 2005): Now a classic book about instincts, intuition, and how you 'know' something; very compatible with expanding your awareness about sensory acuity.

Change Your Brain, Change Your Life, Daniel Amen (Three Rivers Press, 1998): A great book that presents a breakthrough program for conquering anxiety, depression, obsessiveness, anger, and impulsiveness; full of useful tips and techniques.

Chicken Soup For the Soul (and others by the same author/s) Jack Canfield and Mark Victor Hansen (Health Communications Inc., 1993): Heartwarming real-life stories.

Creative Visualizations, Shakti Gawain (Whatever, 1978): Classic, insightful advice on creating the life you want using visualizations and affirmations.

Don't Shoot the Dog, Karen Pryor (Bantam Press, 1984): A slim
paperback with unforgettable stories and research data; essential
principles of learning, based on extensive research of training
animals, dolphins, and children.

Emotional Intelligence, Daniel Goleman (Bantam Doubleday Dell
Publishing Group, 1996): One of the first books to talk about EQ,
why it is important, and some of the brain science that backs
it up. There are now several sequels by the same author (e.g.
Working with Emotional Intelligence).

50 Ways To Let Go and Be Happy, Chuck Spezzano (Coronet, 2001):
One of his many books, with a very practical series of exercises
for letting go; very useful in stubborn cases where forgiveness
is needed.

Happiness Now! Robert Holden (Hodder and Stoughton, 1998):
A message of profound hope and healing all about how to be
happy right now. Robert Holden has also written many other
excellent books.

If It Hurts It Isn't Love by Chuck Spezzano (Mobius, 2001): Insights,
humor, great questions, examples, and exercises to get you
thinking differently about your perspective on relationships. A
lesson for each day of the year; NLP mixed with psychology and
the spiritual principles of *A Course in Miracles*.

Love, an Inner Connection, Carol K. Anthony (Anthony Publishing,
2002): Incredibly insightful and inspirational book about
managing your inner energy, boundaries, and appropriate
behavior. Includes great concepts that work particularly well for
understanding and strengthening the true inner feminine. Linked
to her wonderful book *The Guide to the I Ching*.

Loving What Is, Byron Katie (Harmony Books, 2002): Byron's 'The
WORK' is guaranteed to break through the most stubborn
issues if you are prepared to be honest and do the required
soul searching.

Non Violent Communication, Marshall Rosenberg (Puddledancer
Press, 2001): The full explanation of NVC's approach to creating a
language of compassion; full of great examples and explanations.

Seth Speaks (first book of a series), Jane Roberts (Prentice-Hall, 1974): Amazing insights via the channeled entity 'Seth.' Contains unforgettable, life-changing ideas.

Stop Thinking, Start Living, Richard Carlson (Harper Collins, 1993): Great little book explaining how thoughts determine how you feel and why thinking about problems only makes them worse. Great tips on conquering depression and pessimism, and dismissing negative thoughts to reach inner contentment. Richard Carlson also wrote the bestseller *Don't Sweat the Small Stuff.*

The Path of Least Resistance, Robert Fritz (Fawcett Columbine, 1984): Clearing the path to creativity, this book deals with double binds in an easy-to-understand manner. This will help with decision-making problems.

The 7 Habits of Highly Successful People, Stephen Covey (Simon & Schuster, 1989): A classic book on the inner principles that distinguish extraordinary people and make for great leadership. Good reading for anyone whether in business or not.

The Power of Intention, Dr. Wayne Dwyer (Hay House, 2010): How to train yourself to tune in to source energy and step beyond your mind and ego.

The Seven Principles for Making Marriage Work, John Gottman and Nan Silver (Orion Books, 1999): One of the most enlightening and helpful books about relationships you can ever read. All about non-verbal assumptions, presuppositions, and projections. Great tips on how to heal relationship problems.

Science

The Intention Experiment, Lynne McTaggart (Harper Element, 2008): Great scientific stories and real case histories that show how we are all connected and how our intentions can be harnessed as a force for good.

Molecules of Emotion, Candace Pert (Prentice Hall, 1997): Interesting in-depth information on the brain–body connection via neuropeptide communication.

Spontaneous Evolution, Dr. Bruce Lipton and Steve Bhaerman (Hay House, 2011): Great scientific explanations plus the reasons for changing beliefs so that miraculous healing will occur.

The Biology of Belief, Dr. Bruce Lipton (Hay House, 2011): Essential reading for understanding how the DNA and genes really work, and how you can switch genes on and off by your thinking and beliefs.

The Bond, Lynne McTaggart (Hay House, 2011): How cutting-edge science proves we are in constant relationship with everything and everyone.

The Brain That Changes Itself, Norman Doidge (Penguin, 2008): Fascinating and inspiring research into all kinds of brain dysfunction with stories of how people have healed them.

The Divine Matrix, Gregg Braden (Hay House, 2007): Inspiring, clear descriptions of how new science connects with ancient understandings.

The Field, Lynne McTaggart (Element Books, 2001): Fascinating and historical research explaining scientific theory about gravity, quantum mechanics, field theory, eyesight, healing, intuition, and psychic phenomena.

The Heartmath Solution, Doc Lew Childre, Howard Martin and Donna Beech (HarperOne, 2000): Highly readable, lots of scientific backup about how the heart, brain, and emotions interact and affect our health. Other books on how to apply HeartMath to specific issues such as anger, depression, high blood pressure, etc., are also available.

The Secret Life of the Unborn Child, Dr. Thomas Verney with John Kelly (Sphere Books, 1982): What happens in the womb and life before birth; remarkable true stories give reality to what some people might have difficulty believing.

The Tipping Point, Malcolm Gladwell (Little Brown and Co., 2000): Explanation of how change occurs when events pass the threshold and go over the tipping point.

Interpreting symptoms

Heal Your Body, Louise L. Hay (Hay House, 1982): A small but essential resource encyclopedia of symptoms, probable meanings, and affirmations to heal each one.

The Bodymind Workbook (see also *Your Body Speaks Your Mind*), Debbie Shapiro (Piatkus, 1996): Explains a little about how the tissues of the body become related to our thoughts, feelings, and beliefs; great encyclopedia of body parts and specific health issues give insights about metaphoric significance.

The Healing Power of Illness, Thorwald Dethlefsen and Rüdiger Dahlke (Element, 1983): In-depth exploration of how symptoms are bodily expressions of psychological conflicts.

Working With the Dream Body, Arnold Mindell (Penguin, 1985): An insightful treatise on the meaning behind physical disease, based on the study of dreams and how they can manifest as symptoms.

You Can Heal Your Life, Louise L. Hay (Hay House, 1984): Essential reading! This absolutely classic book details very simply everything you need to know in order to heal anything; includes a short encyclopedia of symptoms and their meanings, many exercises, and affirmations.

Your Body Speaks Your Mind, Debbie Shapiro (Piatkus, 1996): An encyclopedia of body parts in which specific health issues are discussed to give insights about the metaphoric significance.

Healing

Anatomy of the Spirit, Caroline Myss (Bantam, 1997): Fascinating theories and discussion about different paths to healing.

Conscious Medicine, Gill Edwards (Piatkus, 2010): How the mind and body are inseparable; the role of emotions in health and disease and how to transform them.

Dying To Be Me, Anita Moorjani (Hay House, 2012): Anita shares her amazing near-death experience and complete spontaneous remission with the incredible insights she gained.

Forgiveness, Sidney and Suzanne Simon (Warner Books, 1990):
Needing to forgive someone or something is often at the root
of illness. This book offers many frames for thinking about
forgiveness.

Headfirst, Norman Cousins (Penguin, 1989): A conservative yet
interesting book on mind-body processes; how hope, faith,
love, will to live, purpose, and laughter can help combat
medical disease.

Healing Back Pain, Dr. John Sarno (Wellness Central, 2010): An
enlightening book that will have you thinking very differently
about pain and other symptoms in your body. Written by an
orthopedic surgeon working in a hospital, who recommends his
patients NOT to have surgery but, instead, to deal with emotions.

Healing Psyche, Rob van Overbruggen, (BookSurge, LLC, 2006):
A well-documented explanation of psychosomatic medicine,
the mental, emotional, and physical aspects of cancer, and an
explanation of many healing approaches from a specialist in
hypnosis.

Quantum Healing, Deepak Chopra (Bantam, 1989): Written by
a respected endocrinologist and practitioner of Ayurvedic
medicine, this is a very popular book that unites discoveries from
modern physics and molecular biology with spiritually oriented
approaches to healing. Chopra has written many other books on
specific subjects.

Mastering Your Hidden Self, Serge King (Quest Books, 1985): A blend
of modern psychology with spiritual philosophy derived from the
Huna tradition of ancient Hawaii. Contains remarkable parallels
to the presuppositions of NLP.

Radical Forgiveness, Colin C. Tipping (Gateway Press, 2000): Great
insights into the assumptions underlying distress, and how to
work practically with the deeper parts of ourselves.

The Healer Within, Steven Loche and Douglas Colligan (Mentor
Books, 1986): An excellent book describing research into how
certain behavior patterns affect health, including data on specific
diseases.

The Healing Brain, Robert Ornstein and David Sobel (Simon & Schuster, 1987): A plain English account of recent findings showing the direct effect of mood and mind on health, and the emerging science of mood medicine.

The Journey, Brandon Bays (Thorsons, 1999): A very inspirational story about how Brandon healed a huge ovarian cyst and transcended enormous personal challenges and then designed her very helpful healing approach.

Vibrational Medicine, Richard Gerber (Bear & Co., 1988): An extensive compilation of information on human energy systems, which brings scientific theory fully in line with a new paradigm for healing. A classic.

Why Am I Sick? Richard Flook and Rob van Overbruggen (MPG Books, 2008): An NLP and psychological approach to answering questions about depression and illness, explaining the 'meta-medicine solutions' based on new medicine concepts.

You Can't Afford the Luxury of a Negative Thought, John Roger and Peter McWilliams (Prelude Press, 1991): Discussions on how people can acquire 'altitude' on their attitudes about life-threatening illness.

Your Body Believes Every Word You Say, Barbara Levine (Aslan Publishing, 1991): Excellent book on thinking processes, language, and health.

NLP

Awaken the Giant Within, Anthony Robbins (Simon & Schuster, 1991): Tony gives great stories and examples to inspire you about the effectiveness of doing in-depth self-exploration; includes some very insightful exercises.

Beliefs, Robert Dilts, Tim Hallbom and Suzi Smith (Metamorphous Press, 1990): Clear explanations and stories about how beliefs get formed, various types of beliefs, and NLP methods for shifting and changing beliefs.

Core Transformations, Connirae Andreas with Tamara Andreas (Real People Press, 1994): In-depth techniques for spiritual transformation of all kinds of problems and symptoms. Very gentle and compassionate.

Magic of NLP Demystified, Byron A. Lewis and Frank Pucelik (Metamorphous Press, 1982): Interesting examples, stories, and clear descriptions make this basic NLP book a favorite.

Time Line Therapy, Tad James and Wyatt Woodsmall (Meta Publications, 1988): An excellent book that fully explains the theory and practice of visualizing time lines and letting go of negative emotions and limiting decisions.

Spirituality

A Course in Miracles, Anon. (Foundation for Inner Peace; 3 Combined edition 2007 ISBN-10: 1883360242): Radical and transformational book that changes people's lives just by reading it. It is intense. Fully explains the ego mind, which curiously reflects the latest research about quantum physics and the field.

A Return to Love, Marianne Williamson (Harper Collins, 1992): The most useful, easy-to-read and beautiful book that talks from the perspective of *A Course in Miracles* and explains most of the principles in everyday language.

Autobiography of a Yogi, Paramahansa Yogananda (Self Realization Fellowship, 2006): A positively wonderful journey through the life of the 20th-century guru, which will amaze and delight you even if it is written in very flowery English – another world and far ahead of its time.

Conversations with God, Neale Donald Walsch (Hampton Roads, 1993): Questions and answers on important issues almost everyone wants to know about.

How Can I Help? Ram Dass and Paul Gorman (Knopf, 1985): An intimate account of the challenges of a life of service in treating illness and reaching clarity in the midst of suffering.

Radical Forgiveness, Colin C. Tipping (Gill and MacMillan, 2000):
How to explore the hidden assumptions and reach a point of true
forgiveness; the link between forgiveness and healing.

The Isaiah Effect, Gregg Braden (Crown Publications, 2002):
Quantum Science combined with timeless wisdom from the *Dead
Sea Scrolls*; a non-religious, non-denominational form of prayer
to bring healing to our bodies and peace.

The Power of Now, Eckhart Tolle (Hodder & Stoughton, 1999): A
modern gospel that talks down-to-earth transcendental truths
and points us to the portals of the eternal present. There are now
further books by Eckhart as well.

The Reconnection, Dr. Eric Pearl (Hay House, 2001): Insights into
the dynamics of miraculous healing using hands-off imparting of
light to influence the information of the field.

SQ: Spiritual Intelligence, Danah Zohar and Ian Marshall
(Bloomsbury Press, 2000): Holistic approach to understanding
society, quantum theory, and the need for meaning, vision, and
value – which is unique to mankind.

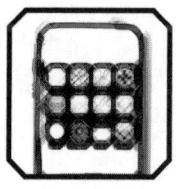
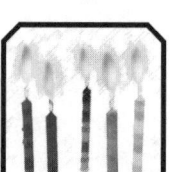

ABOUT THE AUTHOR

Photographer: Tim Spiers

Arielle Essex has worked as an inspirational healer for more than 25 years, practicing various forms of complementary medicine and specializing in mind/body psychology. Creativity and science are her passionate interests. After winning scholarships in art and working as an illustrator for many years, she later went back to school to study osteopathy and naturopathy, graduating top of her class. Because the mind/body connection fascinated her, she expanded her studies to include kinesiology, neuro-linguistic programming (NLP), hypnosis, and many other psychological tools.

As a certified coach and trainer, Arielle also founded the *Practical Miracles* training school, which has provided fully certified and accredited NLP trainings for 17 years. Her story about healing her brain tumor was featured in the recent documentary *The Living Matrix*, which has inspired people all over the world. Arielle combines her knowledge of complementary medicine, NLP, and spiritual healing principles into a path that works. She loves teaching people how to apply these transformative principles and make the choices that heal and build resilience. She is well respected for her individual coaching work, both business and personal, as well as her talks, meditations, books, workshops, and seminars.

arielle_essex

arielle.essex

healing@practicalmiracles.com

www.arielleessex.com